SPIRITUAL MASTERS

Archbishop Emeritus Alfred C. Hughes, S.T.D.

Spiritual Masters

Living and Praying
in the Catholic Tradition

IGNATIUS PRESS   SAN FRANCISCO

Cover art:

Top left
Saint Francis de Sales
Artist and provenance unknown
(public domain)

Top right
Saint Catherine of Siena
by Franceschini Baldassare
(public domain)

Bottom left
Saint Ignatius of Loyola
by Jusepe de Ribera (1591–1652)
(public domain)

Bottom right
Saint Teresa of Avila
by Peter Paul Reubens, circa 1615
© KHM-Museumsverband
Vienna, Austria

Cover design by Riz Boncan Marsella

© 2024 by Ignatius Press
All rights reserved
ISBN 978-1-62164-686-0 (PB)
ISBN 978-1-64229-305-0 (eBook)
Library of Congress Control Number 2023945908
Printed in the United States of America ∞

CONTENTS

ACKNOWLEDGMENTS

No one can write a book alone. Books emerge from communities. This one is rooted in the community of spiritual writers in the Roman Catholic Church.

The eagerness of students at St. John's Seminary in Brighton, Boston, Massachusetts, to learn and appropriate the Catholic spiritual classics first encouraged me to develop a course. Father Aelred Squire's *Asking the Fathers* inspired me in this effort. His acquaintance with the Western spiritual tradition and his ability to retrieve it in an organized way helped to shape the approach I would take.

As the bishop of Baton Rouge, I was privileged to offer a series of public presentations on the Christian classics for interested people. The response of those who participated and their eagerness to secure copies of the classics for their own continued spiritual nourishment encouraged me to consider doing more. A very good friend, Monsignor Cornelius McRae, urged me to explore the possibility of adapting those presentations into a book. That is how the book was conceived.

After preparing a first draft, I tested it with some friends who agreed to read it critically and make suggestions. I am deeply indebted to Monsignor Cornelius McRae, Sister Evelyn Ronan, S.N.D., Ms. Marie Constantin, Ms. Mary Caraway, Mrs. Neola Clark, and Mr. Timothy Basden for the special time and reflective thought they gave in rendering this graced service. Where I was able to incorporate their helpful suggestions, the text was significantly enhanced.

Mrs. Debbie Hebert gave countless hours and painstaking effort to the technical preparation of the manuscript. I stand daily in her debt for her patience, her competence, her attention to detail, and the loving care with which she offered this treasured service.

God grant that this work may in some small way serve his desire to draw us all closer to himself.

INTRODUCTION

A fundamental assumption underlies the message of this book: God offers himself to us all—and the deepest longing of the human heart is for him. We may not be any more aware of this than Augustine was as he was moving through his early journey in life. Augustine eventually came to the point where he could write at the beginning of his *Confessions*: "Our hearts are made for you, O God, and they will not rest until they rest in you."[1]

In our own time, we need to be reminded of the truth of this basic assumption. Religion, which is intended to help direct our restlessness toward communion with God, is instead sometimes ridiculed, often relegated to private life and sometimes inappropriately weaponized in service to military or political goals.

Our increasingly secular culture in the developed world often presents science's claim to truth as undermining the Bible and even faith itself. In fact, the culture in which we live tends to limit truth to scientifically verifiable truth and inclines toward skepticism about our capacity to affirm any objective truth regarding spiritual reality, let alone God.

The narcissistic strand in our culture can make it difficult to develop into true maturity. We can let our egos take over in such a way that we try to assume God's role in ordering life. This can incline us to re-creation of the self, not in the image of God but in our own image. Unbridled

[1] Augustine, *Confessions* I, 1, trans. John Ryan (New York: Doubleday Image, 1960).

sexual drives can lead us to crave sexual gratification as more important than channeling our sexual desires in service to the purpose for which God created them. Gender theory can begin to replace a true Christian anthropology.

When God is not the center of our lives, we can find ourselves not only culturally and politically divided but even inclined to express disagreement violently. The increase in violence and the extreme polarization of society are signs of a society that has lost its way. It is no wonder that many have lost purpose and meaning in life, increasing deaths through cirrhosis of the liver, fentanyl-laced cocaine overdoses, and suicides.

The exodus from Christian churches is alarming. One-third of those baptized have disaffiliated from church faith and practice. For those under thirty, that percentage approaches 50 percent.

When the voice of Christianity is needed most, the Catholic Church seems weakened by the scandal of clergy sexual misconduct, episcopal misjudgments, and relentless media criticism. The Church is on the Cross. Unlike the Lord Jesus, who was nailed to the Cross even though he was without sin, the Church is there because of sin. Victims are angry and many of the faithful are bewildered. Priests are shamed. Trust in bishops is undermined.

In this atmosphere, the Church needs to look both backward and forward. We need to refind the pearl of great price and give up all to reappropriate it. We need to look forward to the future with a confidence born of Gospel living. Whenever scandal has rocked the Church, God has raised up remarkable men and women to model what it means to take the Gospel seriously and become truly generous followers of the Lord.

In the face of all these challenges, people are hungry for inner direction and spiritual meaning. A self-indulgent style of life seems to be running its course. The quest for a spiritual meaning and deeper life is gaining momentum.

The search for the spiritual can move in many disparate directions. The booksellers report the sale of more than a hundred million self-help spiritual books in recent years. Some people look to the East for instruction in Hindu yoga or Zen Buddhist practices. Some have returned to the ancient Babylonian mystic conceptions of the universe with a modernized expression of astrology. Some even tread dangerously in the occult or in devil worship.

Christians can also be led astray. Many have attempted to separate Christ from the Church. Unable to accept a sinful and wounded Church, they seek a spiritual Christ apart from organized Church life.

One of the most encouraging signs is the burgeoning growth of lay ecclesial movements in the Church. Generally speaking, they are happy to accept the life of the Church and explore ways to renew it, drawing on the grace of baptism, the life of the sacraments, prayer, mutual support, and daily practices to promote virtue in the family, the workplace, and the community. These movements are already beginning to impact the wider life of the Church. They are touching the lives of youth and young adults, as is evidenced in their participation in the World Youth Day gatherings.

In addition, the Church experiences other numerous hopeful developments. Recent popes have urged the Church to move from maintenance to mission. We are exploring ways to engage in a new evangelization, new in both aim and means. In addition to continuing missionary outreach to those who have never heard of Christ, the Church is also exploring fruitful ways to reengage the disaffiliated. The digital revolution has opened up new means to utilize in reaching those on the fringe of faith life and practice. Renewal initiatives are underway in the development of parish life encouraging missionary discipleship, catechesis that is more evangelizing, and sacramental participation that is more renewing. Emerging lay associations are encouraging professionals and business leaders to live their faith more intentionally. The Church's engagement in social service to others is becoming more explicit about linking these efforts to the corporal and spiritual works of mercy. The 2021–2024 nurturance of a Eucharistic Revival has been helping the faithful in the United States to be more grounded in sacramental encounter with the Risen Lord. The Church is now, even on the local level, more global and therefore more universal in membership.

In our own day, there is a special need to seek out our spiritual moorings and to avoid anything that suggests a quick fix. All spiritual movements need incorporation in the life of the Church.

A voice from the past can offer salutary counsel to us. In his *Conferences*, John Cassian, who collected many of the sayings of the early ascetics, has handed down to us an enlightening story about Abbot Anthony of Egypt. St. Anthony was approached by some would-be disciples who had found it difficult to decide among themselves what was the most effective way to become a disciple of the Lord. One took the side of fasting; another, long vigils in prayer; and a third, works of charity.

When Anthony was consulted, he acknowledged that there was merit in each of these practices. Then he asked why they thought so many people who had begun the spiritual path with enthusiasm so often collapsed along the way and ended in spiritual confusion or dissipation. The would-be disciples did not know. Anthony suggested that the difficulty might very well be their refusal to accept formation by those who had gone before them. Thus, they never acquired the authentic prudence necessary to bring together the various elements of Christian life in a moderate, faithful, and disciplined response.

We need the experience and the teaching of those who have gone before us. This body of collective wisdom is contained in the classical texts of the common Christian spiritual tradition. Christian spiritual classical literature addresses real life, touches it on a universal plane, and offers a testimony that has been recognized as reliable by the Church. Aelred Squire once wrote: "With a quiet, persistent courtesy the old books insist there is a distinctive pathway to be found in these matters, a 'royal road' which stretches from the days of the Apostles to our own."[2]

Augustine himself in his *Confessions* acknowledged that as a youth he had not known how to read classical literature. He had read the *Aeneid*, but he had not identified with the wandering Aeneas or the weeping Dido. Only after his conversion of life and his newly found appreciation of wisdom literature was he enabled to read classical literature with personal profit. We, too, need help in learning how to read the classics.

We receive helpful guidance in the reading of this kind of literature from the twelfth-century Abbot William of St. Thierry:

> You ought rather to delay with certain minds and grow used to them. For the Scriptures need to be read in the same spirit in which they were written and only in that spirit are they to be understood. You will never reach an understanding of Paul until, by close attention to reading him and the application of continual reflection, you imbibe his spirit. You will never arrive at understanding David until by actual experience you realize what the

[2] Aelred Squire, *Asking the Fathers* (London: S.P.C.K., 1973), 4.

psalms are about. So it is with the rest. In every piece of Scripture, real attention is as different from mere reading as friendship is from entertainment or the love of a friend from a casual greeting.[3]

This final sentence bears repeating: "Real [or spiritual] attention is as different from mere reading [and certainly speed reading] as friendship is from entertainment or the love of a friend from a casual greeting."

Much of today's education and learning seem to produce considerable boredom. Is not this boredom related to a lack of interior experience? When interiorly we are not engaged with what we are doing exteriorly, we are bored. To the extent that our learning is not accompanied by an interior thirst for truth and understanding, we are going to experience ourselves as bombarded with facts and figures. We have to bring a sense of wonder and awe to learning and to life if we are going to be truly engaged in the experience. This is particularly important in coming to spiritual reading and to worship. For wisdom is far more important than knowledge!

Sacred reading, then, is the holy practice of pondering classical texts that speak to us about God and trying to respond to him in life. Sacred Scripture offers us the example of men and women who struggled to say yes to God. Spiritual writers record for us the example of the saints. When they present to us real-life persons and are realistic about the challenges of life, they inspire us and help us to take seriously the challenges before us.

A further and even more important task is to understand *how* to approach reading sacred classical literature. Entering into spiritual reading in a life-giving way is a true art. We need to take off *the student hat* and put on *the*

---

[3] William of St. Thierry (*PL* 184, Col. 327–28).

disciple hat. This involves more dwelling and less digging. It involves less analyzing and more of a desire to be inspired or moved to change our lives. We need to bring our inner and deeper selves to the effort.

Obviously, it will be important to be realistic about the historically conditioned elements in the reading we may do. For example, the imagery of castle life in St. Teresa of Ávila or the suspicion about intellectual study in *The Imitation of Christ* may initially put us off. If we understand the time period in which they were written and focus on the life-giving truth they communicate, God will use this effort to open up deeper understanding and facilitate richer spiritual life.

Pondering classical spiritual texts should not lead to a false kind of perfectionism. What the authentic spiritual writers point to most is realism about the living of our lives on a deeply personal and fruitful level. What is important is allowing the Holy Spirit to touch the depths of the human heart.

In the chapters of this book, I will try to present significant themes in the living of the Christian spiritual life by drawing on the rich teaching of some of the Western spiritual classics. The themes will build on one another.[4] It is my hope that by locating the spiritual classics in their historical setting it will be possible to invite you to read these classics with understanding and apply them to your own life experiences. By being introduced to a number of the classics, it may be possible to appreciate the richness of this tradition and the depth of meaning of the spiritual life God calls us to live in Christ Jesus as we live in this third millennium of Christianity.

[4] For the themes of the spiritual life, see Aelred Squire, *Asking the Fathers*. Squire's book has had a profound impact on the development of this writer's work.

When we want to take the spiritual life seriously, it is important to begin where we are and to introduce into our lives some extended moments of solitude. For this we turn to St. Anthony of the Desert. We cannot sustain moments of solitude very long without realizing the need to clarify who we are and where we are going. Walter Hilton and his *Scale of Perfection* help us address this. The question of our identity and mission brings with it the realization that something has gone wrong in the world and in our own lives. For this we turn to Augustine and his *Confessions*. In order to address the central driving force in the spiritual life, we turn to Aelred of Rievaulx to help us explore the meaning of Christian charity.

The deepening awareness of God, our own identity and purpose, and our work in the world lead us to develop a pattern of life that supports Christian discipleship. Since St. Benedict did this for his disciples, we will look to him for hints for a rhythm of life for ourselves.

Serious engagement with the Christian spiritual life inevitably leads us to confront serious obstacles. The journey is not smooth. It involves a real struggle. *The Imitation of Christ*, usually attributed to Thomas à Kempis, will help us develop realism about this struggle.

We will turn to explicit treatment of prayer after discussing these fundamental issues of our identity, destiny, vocation, and struggles. Guigo the Carthusian will guide us into understanding the goal of prayer and a blessed means for listening to the Word of God. Teresa of Ávila's *Way of Perfection* will help us appreciate the way prayer is related to real life. Catherine of Siena will help us recognize the deeper meaning of public prayer and sacramental life.

Prayer bears fruit in the life of virtue. St. Francis de Sales in his *Introduction to the Devout Life* will be our guide to personal virtue. St. Ignatius of Loyola will help us grow in understanding social virtue. We will inevitably face suffering. As a matter of fact, we will often experience suffering as an obstacle to the spiritual life. St. John of the Cross will unveil for us the way in which suffering can lead us to God. Finally, we will focus on the ultimate goal of our lives, and Jean-Pierre de Caussade will help us focus on it.

The issues addressed in each chapter will inevitably overlap in the living of human life. However, the order chosen in this book reflects the usual timing and readiness that we experience in giving more attention to the issues involved. As you read the book, you may be helped by moving on to the chapter that directly addresses the questions that have emerged for you in your journey to God.

I invite you to read this book slowly and pause when God may draw you to ponder a word or a thought. The book is written for prayerful reading. May this effort be an instrument of God's grace for you.

CHAPTER 1

Taking Christian Life Seriously

Anthony and Desert Solitude

Who takes the Christian spiritual life seriously? Is the richness of this life open to the *ordinary* Christian? Where do we begin? How do we take the first step? Perhaps we can learn from those who have gone before us.

In the immediate generations following the death and Resurrection of the Lord, Christian disciples faced radical questions in life. They were constantly exposed to the possibility of public ridicule or even persecution and death. The decision to follow Christ was not taken lightly. Individuals and families who accepted the call took the living of the new way very seriously.

Since the first three centuries of persecution, Christians have not always had to face the same kind of radical decision because of external hostility. With diminished external challenge, Christians have often accepted uncritically the ways of the world. This has always rightfully left some people uneasy. Can we learn from those who first faced this at the end of the period of the early persecutions?

The Movement to Solitude

In the fourth and fifth centuries, there was considerable social upheaval. The Roman Empire was beginning to dissolve. Existing political structures were collapsing. Even non-Christians were beginning to see that their world, including the spiritual world, was in disarray.

In this atmosphere, Anthony of Egypt sensed a call in the year 269 to emulate the apostles and abandon everything in order to follow the Lord. One day as he was at Mass in his local parish church, he heard the Gospel reading echo the words of the Lord in response to a rich man who asked Jesus what he must do to inherit eternal life: "You are lacking in one thing. Go, sell what you have, give to the poor and you will have treasure in heaven; then come, follow me" (Mk 10:21).

Anthony rejected the increasingly sophisticated and routine Christianity of the third-century Mediterranean villages and towns and reasserted the primitive idea that conversion meant a radical discontinuity in life.

Anthony, who lived to be more than a hundred years old, and some others became desert hermits for life. But most went into the desert for only briefer periods of time. People from the villages used to go out to seek the counsel of those who spent some time in the desert. The *sayings* of these desert people were then pondered as possible directives for life.

The monk Pachomius began to gather some of the second-generation hermits into the first monastic foundation. At the end of his life, he left two monasteries of women and nine monasteries of men. He also developed a rule of life that became a directive for the early monks. Eventually, Basil, who lived in the fourth century, built on the work of Pachomius and wrote his Rules, which ultimately became the foundation of Eastern monasticism.

These pioneers of a more radical living of the Christian life had considerable impact on the ordinary people who witnessed what happened to them. People went out to the desert to visit them. They found that the desert had become a place of solitude where some men and women were discovering who they really were. They had begun to recognize better who God is—not as he initially seemed to be. They also developed a more realistic understanding of themselves—not as they had originally imagined themselves to be. They came to appreciate the world as it is—fundamentally good, yet corrupted by sin. They also came to acknowledge the reality of the demonic.

These people entered into a process of *recognition*. This knowledge had been deep within them but not yet brought to a conscious level. They learned through experience to reflect on creation and to ponder God's word. Those who entered the desert began to recognize that if their attitude toward the least of God's creatures was wrong, then their attitude toward God would become wrong. They began to recognize how prejudices within them led them to censor some dimensions of the world, the teaching of the Bible, and finally even God himself. They came to acknowledge the significance of truly being interiorly alive.

For those who went there, the desert had become a place where people were recognizing the truth that life is a gift from God—not our own. They learned to accept help from others who had tested themselves with extended experience in order to find the right way to live it. They discovered a need to embrace certain conditions in life in order to come to the experiential life-giving truth that God reveals. The one who lives a certain kind of life is the one who is in a position to understand God's revelation.

God is always revealing himself; the obstacles, however, are within us. The men and women who entered the desert were skeptical about those who turned away from the Church because they were dissatisfied with what they found. They had come to recognize that the obstacles we think are outside of us are usually within us. It is only in addressing them that disciples are then freed to find again the true God, the true Church, the true world, and the ultimate meaning of life.

The Teaching from Solitude

As people went into the desert to consult these desert pioneers, they began to record some of the cryptic responses that these spiritual giants offered to them. Only in the mid-fifth century was a serious effort made to collect these sayings.

Thomas Merton brought together a very brief selection of some of these sayings in his *Wisdom of the Desert*. In reading these sayings, it is important to note that we are dealing with literature that is commonly referred to as wisdom literature. These sayings reveal deeper truths. Some are short precepts or maxims. For example: "An elder said: A man who keeps death before his eyes will at all times overcome his cowardice."[1]

Some are folk sayings in the form of metaphors or similes: "Abbot Pastor said: A man must breathe humility and the fear of the Lord just as ceaselessly as he inhales or exhales the air" (82).

Some are parables:

Once they asked Abbot Agatho: "Which is greater? Bodily asceticism or watchfulness over the interior man?" The

[1] Thomas Merton, trans., *The Wisdom of the Desert: Sayings from the Desert Fathers of the Fourth Century* (New York: New Directions, 1970), 138. Subsequent quotations are from this edition and will be cited in the text.

elder said: "A man is like a tree. His bodily works are like the leaves of the tree. But interior self-custody is like the fruits. Since, then, it is written that every tree not bearing good fruit shall be cut down and cast into the fire, we must take all care to bear this fruit which is custody of the mind. But we also need leaves to cover and adorn us: and that means good works done with the aid of the body." (114)

We need to read such literature in a spirit of prayerful pondering of the text to discover the deeper meaning. We need to invoke the light of the Holy Spirit. We are dealing with sayings that interpret human experience. They presume that one is living a certain kind of life in order to grow in understanding of the way of life rooted in the Gospel. The words are simple, honest, without affectation. They must be received by people who are willing to be challenged and changed. The words come from people who are of few words. Those who went to seek their advice tended to approach them with words such as these: "What is so good that I may do it and live?" or "Speak to me a word that I may live."

The words that the desert pioneers spoke address basic realities of the interior struggle to live a truly Christian life: humility, charity, meekness, discretion, self-denial, and common sense. They were particularly interested in urging the Christian disciple to realize the truth about his very self. They insisted on the need to be faithful to solitude. They urged a focus simply on what God is asking personally and uniquely in life:

A brother asked one of the elders: "What good thing shall I do and have life thereby?" The old man replied: "God alone knows what is good. However, I have heard it said that someone inquired of Father Abbot Nisteros the Great, the friend of Abbot Anthony, asking: 'What good shall

I do?' And that he replied: 'Not all works are alike. The Scripture says that Abraham was hospitable and God was with him. Elias loved solitary prayer and God was with him. And David was humble and God was with him.' Therefore whatever you see your soul to desire according to God, do that thing and you shall keep your heart safe." (3)

These solitaries were insistent upon humility: "Yet another elder said if you see a young monk by his own will climbing up into heaven, take him by the foot and throw him on the ground, because what he is doing is not good for him" (62).

These ancient spiritual giants were equally insistent that anger should not take over in our lives: "Abbot Macarius said: 'If wishing to correct another you are moved to anger you gratify your own passion. Do not lose yourself in order to save another'" (18).

They pointed out the need to work and the need for leisure:

It was told of Abbot John the Dwarf that once he had said to his older brother: "I want to live in the same security as the angels have, doing no work, but serving God without intermission." In casting off everything he had on, he started out into the desert. When a week had gone by he returned to his brother. While he was knocking on the door his brother called out before opening and asked: "Who are you?" He replied: "I am John." Then his brother answered and said: "John has become an angel and is no longer among men." But John kept on knocking and said: "It is I." Still the brother did not open but kept him waiting. Finally opening the door he said: "If you are a man, you are going to have to start working again in order to live. But if you are an angel, why do you want to come into a cell?" So John did penance and said: "Forgive me, brother, for I have sinned." (45)

This is to be balanced with the following saying of St. Anthony:

> Once Abbot Anthony was conversing with some brethren and a hunter who was after game in the wilderness came upon them. He saw Abbot Anthony and the brothers enjoying themselves and disapproved. Abbot Anthony said: "Put an arrow in your bow and shoot it." This he did. "Now shoot another," said the elder. "And another. And another." The hunter said: "If I bend the bow all the time it will break." Abbot Anthony replied: "So it is also in the work of God. If we push ourselves beyond measure the brethren will soon collapse. It is right therefore from time to time to relax their efforts." (106)

These men and women who became great spiritual directors were equally concerned about urging disciples of the Lord to seek the truth about others: "One of the brethren had sinned and the priest told him to leave the community. So then Abbot Paphnutius got up and walked out with him saying, 'I, too, am a sinner'" (40).

They insisted on compassion in judging the actions of others. They also wanted the disciples to extend hospitality:

> A brother came and stayed with a certain solitary. When he was leaving he said: "Forgive me, father, for I have broken in upon your rule." But the hermit replied saying: "My rule is to receive you with hospitality and to let you go in peace." (75)

These desert solitaries warned against the sin of detraction, that is, speaking ill of another: "Abbot Hyperchius said: 'It is better to eat meat and drink wine, than by detraction to devour the flesh of your brother'" (19).

They saw competitiveness and greed as the root of conflicts with others:

There were two elders living together in a cell and they
had never had so much as one quarrel with one another.
One therefore said to the other: "Come on. Let us have
at least one quarrel like other men." The other said:
"I don't know how to start a quarrel." The first said: "I
will take this brick and place it here between us. Then
I will say it is mine. After that, you will say that it is yours.
This is what leads to a dispute and a fight." So then they
placed the brick between them. One said: "It is mine"
and the other replied to the first: "I do believe it is mine."
The first one said again: "It is not yours, it is mine." So the
other answered: "Well, if it is yours, take it." Thus they
did not manage after all to get into a quarrel. (112)

It was after developing a reliable way of seeking truth
about themselves and about others that the desert folk
identified the conditions in their life for seeking the truth
about God. For them it was extraordinarily important to
prefer silence in their lives in order to give room for God
to speak to them:

One of the elders used to say: "In the beginning when we
got together, we used to talk about something that was
good for our souls and we went up and up and ascended
even to heaven. But now we get together and spend our
time in criticizing everything and we drag one another
down into the abyss." (61)

They also considered it important to develop stability
in life and place of residence: "An elder said: 'Just as a tree
cannot bear fruit if it is often transplanted, so neither can a
monk bear fruit if he frequently changes his abode'" (27).

The desert monks found themselves recognizing more
clearly the truth about the world. Anthony of the Desert is
quoted as saying: "My book, O philosopher, is the nature

of created things and it is present when I will for me to read the words of God" (17).

They also urged an appropriate renunciation and detachment with regard to the world's goods.

In the disciplined way of life that these desert people embraced, they recognized the reality and power of the demonic. They saw themselves as engaged in a war from which they could not shy away. They needed to recognize the existence of the devil:

> Another of the elders said: "When the eyes of an ox or mule are covered, then he goes round and round turning the mill wheel. But if his eyes are uncovered, he will not go around in the circle of the mill wheel. So, too, the devil if he manages to cover the eyes of a man, he can humiliate him in every sin. But if that man's eyes are not closed he can easily escape from the devil." (66)

For them virtue was ultimately revealed only in triumph over temptation: "Abbot Pastor said: 'The virtue of a monk is made manifest by temptations'" (25).

Implications for Us

Obviously, we find ourselves in a different place in living in the third millennium. As indicated in the introduction, we face new challenges, new opportunities. The superficial voices that engulf us tend to keep us from becoming sufficiently centered to focus on the deeper questions of life. Our lives are far more complicated, intense, and demanding. We cannot escape from the many challenges that press upon us.

The wisdom of the desert, however, reminds us that we, too, need to find a desert place in our own lives in order to move into deeper life. If we want to take spiritual living seriously, we need to find a place where we can experience solitude on a regular basis. It is only there that we can *recognize* the life-giving truth about God, ourselves, others, the world, and the devil. It is only in fidelity to this practice that we can really sense where we may be in the journey of life.

For most of us, the greatest challenge will be to find a place and a time that will provide a reasonable expectation of solitude for us. The busyness of our lives, the unexpected demands that press upon us, and the competing messages that engulf us make this a challenge. There is a special advantage in rising early enough in the morning to ensure a time of quiet before the day begins in earnest. If we are able to do this, it will have a more enduring impact upon the rest of our day. Circumstances may also dictate taking time away in the course of the day or late in the evening. What is important is that it is a time when we can rely on being relatively uninterrupted.

As we begin to have a regular time of solitude, the greatest temptation is going to be to give it up. The initial attempts will most probably encounter inner resistance. We may call into question the value of the time even when we are successful in providing for it. Until habits in support of it are in place, we will find it a significant struggle.

In the selection of the location, it will be helpful to find a place that gives us a sense of God's presence. Some will find the Eucharistic presence particularly supportive of such prayer. Others will be more encouraged by a view of nature. For others it may be a corner of the house where a crucifix or an image of the Lord or a lighted candle or burning incense is supportive of quiet presence.

The devil himself is going to try to dissuade us from embracing this practice. He knows that fidelity to solitude is going to do more to expose his wiles and support openness to God than anything else. This discipline will help us deepen an attentiveness and a responsiveness to the desire for God within us. It is in solitude that we will become more aware of the competitive desires and drives that need to be attended to if we are to make progress in the Christian spiritual life. Most of all, it is in this quiet that we will begin to deepen the desire that God has planted within us.

Lord Jesus, help me to find a special time and place for you in my daily life. I tend to be so busy and so preoccupied. I neglect to provide the opportunity simply to be with you. Even when I do set aside time for prayer, I tend to become so distracted. The concerns and anxieties that trouble me tend to well up and occupy my attention. Give me the courage to weather the storm of my inner desires, drives, and fear so that I can become faithful to quiet time with you. Enable me in this time to experience more clearly the truth about you, about me, about others, about the world, about the devil. Sustain me in a loving embrace of all that is truly real. Amen.

CHAPTER 2

Who Are We?

Walter Hilton and the Image of God

If we take the call to solitude seriously, we will begin to move beyond the cacophony of messages that ordinarily deafen us and begin to encounter reality as it truly is: God, ourselves, others, the world, and the demonic. As this begins to happen and as we embark on this spiritual journey, it will be important to clarify our understanding of the nature and destiny of the human person. For help with this, let us turn to the fourteenth-century spiritual director Walter Hilton.

Walter Hilton and His Period

The fourteenth century was a century of transition. The whole structure of society was changing. People felt very vulnerable. The Black Plague laid claim to the lives of more than a third of the population in Europe. The spirit of nationalism was rampant. An on-again, off-again war that lasted more than a hundred years was a terribly unfortunate by-product of this nationalistic spirit in England and France. Tax money was spent for waging war, not for assisting the poor. The people became disenchanted with governmental policies. A rise in the development of vernacular languages increased the nationalistic tendencies. In England the peasants revolted in 1381 and brought for the first time the people's voice into the government in that country.

This century was also marked by considerable church-state tension. A legal struggle ensued in a number of countries between crown and pope over the appointment of bishops. There was considerable antipapal feeling in England because of the pope's move to Avignon in 1309. Neither society nor the Church seemed to offer stability in depth of life.

In this atmosphere, Walter Hilton lived and died. We know very little about him. He was probably born in Yorkshire, England. He was ordained a priest and studied canon law, possibly at Cambridge University. He became a solitary for a period of time. Then he emerged from seclusion to enter the Thurgarton Priory as a canon of St. Augustine in the 1380s. He died in 1395.

Walter Hilton must have been a strong person, able to stand alone in a time of great turmoil. He had a predilection for anonymity and the hidden life. He resisted the intellectual tendencies of Oxford University, with its philosophical approach championed by William Ockham and the theological emphasis led by John Duns Scotus. Without succumbing to their errors, he tried to foster in his teaching and way of life a concern for the poor that John Wycliffe and the Lollards promoted. He was marked by prudence and good judgment in offering spiritual direction to others. He left behind lengthy letters of spiritual direction, a few brief scriptural commentaries, a polemical work in defense of the use of images in prayer, and a lengthy manual for solitaries called *The Scale of Perfection*.

The Teaching of *The Scale of Perfection*

Walter Hilton presented in *The Scale of Perfection* a doctrine that is central to the spiritual teaching in the Christian tradition. It is sometimes called the "image doctrine" because it is an exposition of the meaning of the scriptural affirmation that human beings have been created in God's image and likeness. This teaching provides an understanding of the human person, drawn from Sacred Scripture.

Hilton was a faithful exponent of the Christian view of the human person as a creature made with a special dignity in the image and likeness of God, tarnished by sin but restored by redemption. He described the spiritual journey for the Christian in three stages: that of the beginning soul; that of the profiting soul; and that of the perfect soul that is reformed in faith and feeling.

Hilton described the initial stage in the Christian life as the transformation of the image of sin, which each one of us inherits, into a reform in faith. Through baptism, the basic image of God in which the human person has been created, but which has been distorted by the fall and subsequent personal sin, is reformed in sacrament. A change really takes place, even though we do not yet experience it. We know it only by faith.

The person who takes the spiritual life seriously becomes a profiting soul. As we begin to live our baptismal life more consciously, we then move into the spiritual journey. This journey demands a significant purification. It begins with enlivening the desire for God and recognizing there is one principal goal in life. Hilton described it in this way:

> A man once wished to go to Jerusalem, and since he did not know the way, he called on another man who, he hoped, knew the way, and asked him for information. This other man told him that he would not reach it without great

hardship and effort. "The way is long," he said, "and there is great danger from thieves and bandits, as well as many other difficulties which beset a man on this journey. Furthermore there are many different roads which seem to lead towards it, but every day men are killed and robbed, and never reach their goal. But I can guarantee one road which will lead you to the city of Jerusalem if you will keep to it. On this road your life will be safe, but you will have to undergo robbery, violence and great distress."[1]

In this passage, Hilton attempted to express in parable form the significance of a burning desire for God and for following the life and teaching of Jesus, no matter what the obstacles may be.

Hilton described growth in prayer as beginning with the repetition of vocal prayers, moving toward a more meditative and affective prayer, and finally developing into a greater prayer of rest. He spoke of a night in which the person moves from a false day or light through darkness (suffering) to a real day. This involves an active struggle with sin, especially the roots of sin and the accompanying mortification and spirit of compunction needed. Fundamentally, he insisted, however, that it is God's initiative that makes it possible.

Hilton was realistic about the difficulties that we experience in attempting to be faithful to this journey. In reading this, it is important to interpret the Middle English term "feeling" as referring to "experience":

I think one reason why people are so seldom reformed in feeling is that many who have been reformed in faith do not make a wholehearted effort to grow in grace, or

[1] Walter Hilton, *The Scale of Perfection* II, 29, trans. Leo Sherley-Price (St. Meinrad, Ind.: Abbey Press, 1975). Subsequent quotations are from this edition and will be cited in the text.

to lead better lives by means of earnest prayer and meditation, and by other spiritual and bodily exercises. They
think it sufficient to avoid mortal sin, and to continue to
live in the same way. They say that it is enough for them
to be saved, and they are content with the lowest place in
heaven, wanting nothing higher. (II, 18)

Hilton mentioned another reason: "Some who are
reformed in faith adopt a certain rule of life in both spiritual and worldly matters in the early days of their conversion, and imagine that they must always observe it
without change, even though grace may reveal a better
[rule]" (II, 19).

In those words, Hilton wanted to warn against letting
any discipline of life become an end in itself, rather than a
condition for openness and receptivity to God.

The third stage of development, as described in *The
Scale of Perfection*, belongs to that of the perfect soul. It
involves a contemplative experience, affecting the whole
person. Hilton described it as a gradual growth in reform
in faith and feeling. It is marked by a much clearer experience of God's initiative: "In this peace God reveals himself
to the soul, sometimes as Lord to be feared, sometimes as
a Father to be reverenced, and sometimes as a Spouse to
be loved" (II, 44).

This stage is marked by special grace. The senses become
more intuitively responsive to God, and the whole person
becomes deepened in the living of the Christian moral and
spiritual life.

The Image Doctrine

As we try to appreciate the teaching of Walter Hilton we
are reminded that the view that we take of our humanity

has profound implications for the way in which we live our lives. The view of New York's Madison Avenue or of mass media, for instance, tends to promote a narcissism or consumerism. The view of male chauvinism is that woman is innately inferior to man. The view of radical feminism is that woman has the ultimate control over her own life and body. The view of racism is that one race, usually the white race, is superior to other races. The view of a new biologism is that we can manufacture life apart from procreation and predetermine the characteristics of our offspring through the manipulation of human genes.

Christians have asked themselves, not what do we think of ourselves, but how does God see us. The answer that revelation gives is that God has created us in his image and likeness. This is revealed to us is in the first chapter of the Book of Genesis, verses 26–27:

> Then God said: "Let us make man in our image, after our likeness; and let them have dominion over the fish of the sea, and over the birds of the air, and over the cattle, and over all the earth, and over every creeping thing that creeps upon the earth." So God created man in his image, in the image of God he created him; male and female he created them.

It is celebrated in the Psalms. The prophets witnessed to it and chided the Israelites whenever they substituted another image for the image of God in the human person.

In the New Testament, St. Paul identified Jesus Christ as "the image of the invisible God" (Col 1:15). He also indicated that every true disciple has been "predestined to be conformed to the image of his Son" (Rom 8:29). "And we all, with unveiled face, beholding the glory of the Lord, are being changed into his likeness from one degree of glory to another; for this comes from the Lord who is the Spirit" (2 Cor 3:18).

Over the centuries, spiritual writers have sought to explore what this image teaching in Sacred Scripture might ultimately mean. Irenaeus taught that all human beings find their ultimate identity in Jesus Christ. Tertullian witnessed to the truth that God's image within us has remained even after the fall, but our likeness to him was lost through sin. Clement and Origen further expanded this teaching. Basil, Gregory of Nyssa, and Gregory Nazianzus interpreted the spiritual life as a gradual reappropriation of the likeness that is rooted in our creation in the image of God.

Augustine located the image of God in the human heart, mind, and will. The Cistercians Bernard, William of St. Thierry, and Aelred of Rievaulx further developed this theme. Thomas Aquinas included it in his *Summa Theologiae*. The French school of spirituality of the seventeenth and eighteenth centuries developed extensive teaching on this. It is referred to in the Second Vatican Council's Pastoral Constitution on the Church in the Modern World. Pope St. John Paul II included it in his first encyclical, *The Redeemer of Man* and Pope Francis in *Evangelii Gaudium*.

Common threads are woven into the teaching of these various witnesses to the meaning of Sacred Scripture. They taught that the original image of God found in the human person is, as Augustine expressed it so vividly, revealed in the human heart, the intellect, and the will. For these writers, the heart is not the physiological organ of the body that we call the heart, nor is it the seat of human emotions. Rather, the heart is the seat of unity, direction, purpose, and desire in the human person. It is in the heart that appropriation, integration, and centering takes place. This, they taught, seems to be reflective of God the Father—the origin, source of order and purpose, the destiny of the human race.

The mind provides us with the capacity to know, not only rationally but also suprarationally. We therefore have the capacity for intuition and *recognition*, the appreciation of truths that seem to be deeply embedded in human consciousness and gradually have to be brought to light. When we lay hold of life-giving truth, it is almost as if the truth had previously been latent in our subconscious. The Church writers referred to this experience as reminiscence. For them the mind is the human faculty that enables us to do this and, thus, is an image of God the Son, who perfectly knows the Father and reveals him to us.

The human will provides us with the capacity to make a gift of ourselves totally, permanently, and faithfully. It provides us not merely with the capacity for willpower, but the ability to live for others and to be able to make a permanent gift of ourselves to others. According to these writers, the will is the image of God the Holy Spirit, perfect and eternal gift of the Father to the Son and the Son to the Father.

This image of God within us, the spiritual writers taught, was distorted by the original sin of our first parents. We are born into this condition. It is beyond our human personal responsibility and somehow we hand it on to our descendants. We experience that our hearts are divided, disoriented, and hardened as St. Paul testified (see Rom 7:13–20).

Our minds are darkened and are inclined to fall victim to deceit. The Lord Jesus testified that the Evil One was the author of deceit (see Jn 8:44). Our wills are weakened, in conflict, and powerless (see Rom 7:18–20; 2 Cor 12:7–10).

Jesus Christ has restored the likeness to the image of God in us. He not only revealed the true image, but he made the restoration of this image possible for us. He has done this objectively for us in the way in which he lived his life. His heart revealed a unity of purpose, meaning, self-awareness, and a desire to live for the Father in the Holy Spirit (see Heb 10:5–7). His mind understood the Father's message and expressed it for us all. His will was utterly committed to making a gift of himself even in the face of severe human reluctance. This was dramatically displayed in the agony in the Garden of Gethsemane.

What Jesus Christ effected in principle for the restoration of the likeness of the image of God within us becomes ours in sacrament through baptism and confirmation. We are incorporated into the restored image of Jesus Christ through these sacraments. Christ's life, message, and mission as authentically interpreted by the Church are made reliably available to us. Then in the experience of living Christian life, we embrace the spiritual journey leading toward an ever-greater restoration of our likeness to God. For this to happen, it is important to activate the desire for God. It is important to want to be taught by God's revelation. It is important to introduce the conditions for self-giving love, including conversion and growth in virtue. It is important to imitate Jesus Christ.

Implications for the Christian Spiritual Life

How difficult it is to overestimate the significance of the image doctrine in Christian teaching!

The understanding of the human person that implicitly undergirds the way we live our life has a profound impact on the way we live. If, for instance, we think of ourselves as individualistic, autonomous human persons, we will try to live very independent and selfish lives. If we think of ourselves as persons with only bodily needs, we will attempt to live for our bodies alone. If we think that as human persons we realize our greatest potential when we experience great success or acclaim or power, we will aspire to realize those goals. If we consider the manufacturing of offspring with the genes most personally valued or the indefinite prolongation of our own human lives of principal human concern, then we will seek to exploit discoveries in biological research without much of any reference to God. But if we realize that our greatest dignity is in coming to know God in a truly experiential and life-giving way, to love him and through this love to make a gift of ourselves to him for others, this will have a profound impact on the way in which we approach our decisions in life.

As we move into a regular experience of solitude, we need to ask ourselves which understanding of the human person motivates us. Do we recognize that it is the image of God within us that gives profound dignity to the human person and reveals our destiny?

The noblest activities of the human person are to know and to love. We are called to know and love on every level of our being. When we know life-giving truth not only with the mind but also with the heart, and love goodness with the mind as well as the will, we are truly drawn to the good, the true, and the beautiful. We are drawn to God. All creatures reveal his face in part but always fall short. Each day of life in this world we are invited to recognize this face of God in all that happens. There is no greater happiness available to us than knowing and loving God amidst the vicissitudes of this life so as to live in communion with him forever in the next.

As we persevere in fidelity to solitude in our life, we will begin to recognize more fully the image of sin that is at work within us. What are the real divisions in our own hearts? What is the darkness or the confusion that continues to obscure life-giving truth in our lives? What are the weaknesses that undermine our capacity to make a more long-range gift of ourselves in life? This perseverance in solitude helps us then to move into a conversion of heart that is God-inspired and truly free.

We are to turn to Jesus Christ as the perfect image of the Father. It is ours to explore ways to encourage the desire for him to become more and more paramount in our lives. We also want to deepen the receptivity in our own understanding so that we can accept his teaching directives for our lives. Under his grace, we want the capacity to make a more lasting gift of ourselves become the ultimate purpose of our lives. The dignity and sacredness of every human life is rooted in this teaching.

Lord Jesus, how marvelously we are made! We have come from the Father and we are to return to him. We realize this by becoming incorporated in you in the Church in this life. Help me to desire you above all. I want to know the truth you reveal and to live that truth in love. I want to belong to you above all. Draw me beyond my limited desires, understanding, and love. Make possible within me what I cannot do on my own. Amen.

CHAPTER 3

Something's Wrong

Augustine Discovers Sin

Any attempt to incorporate regular solitude into life begins to open up for us times of exterior quiet. However, when we reduce external stimuli, we may face so much inner turmoil that we are tempted to give up solitude altogether. We become more and more conscious of the noise that is within. These are the impulsive and compulsive drives at work. They feed our imagination, our feelings, and our thoughts. In fact, we may find it almost impossible to sustain any interior quiet because these interior movements are so strong. We can become easily discouraged and begin to think that we are wasting our time as we try to persevere in solitude.

We should not be surprised to recognize that the image of the glory in which we have been created and into which we are called is in sharp contrast with the painful experience of daily life. We are continually reminded that something has gone unmistakably wrong with the world and with ourselves. To help us understand this better we turn now to Augustine of Hippo.

The Life and Times of Augustine

Augustine lived in the second half of the fourth century and the first third of the fifth. The Roman world was courting disaster. Hordes of tribes were attacking the empire from the north. Taxation in the Roman Empire had doubled and then tripled in support of the army for protection. In the process, government had become very remote from the people.

The Church was making its own transition from the life of persecution to a more ordinary life. It was obvious that the removal of external danger meant that the motivation for taking discipleship more seriously had to come from within.

Augustine was born in 354 in Tagaste, in what is now Algeria. His father was poor, uneducated, and led a life that left something to be desired. His mother, Monica, was a very influential figure in his life. She was dignified, a strong believer in good education, and a faithful Christian. Augustine had a brother and probably two sisters.

Initially, Augustine was not drawn to education, but he showed significant promise even from his early years. When Augustine's father found enough money, he sent him to Carthage to further his education. Here Augustine experienced the freedom of the big city. In a real adolescent crisis, he fell *in love with love*, as he himself described it. He became sexually active. His father died at the end of Augustine's first year of study and this catapulted the young man into a period of great personal turmoil. Augustine felt that he had never really known his father and that his father had never really understood him.

Augustine testified that his first conversion took place when he was nineteen. It was a conversion of the mind through his reading of Cicero's *Hortensius*. The young man was fired from within to seek wisdom, not just knowledge.

He was encouraged to seek the meaning of life, the universe, evil. In retrospect he recognized that it was a kind of religious quest that had been awakened in him.

Augustine had to decide what form his pursuit of wisdom would take. Although he had never been baptized, his mother had tried to offer him a formation in Christian faith. Augustine looked to the Bible to seek the teaching of wisdom. What he found instead was the Word-made-flesh—suffering and crucified. Moreover, and unfortunately, the Latin translations available in his time were unbelievably bad and contrasted poorly with the secular classical literature he had thus far been studying. So he became disenchanted with the biblical route.

Augustine then found a group of intelligent, articulate believers who claimed to lead people to a more direct, "less ridiculous" understanding of God. They appealed to reason and compelled attention and admiration by their demanding style of life. The central figure for them was Christ, the enlightener, the teacher of wisdom, the one sent to awaken us to the divinity within ourselves. These people were called Manichaeans. They were a group of elect who lived rigorously, exuded an air of mystery, hinted at a knowledge of deeper secrets, and even suggested that they had an answer to the problem of evil. Augustine was to stay with the Manichaeans for nine years until he finally had a disastrous encounter with one of their most revered teachers, Faustus. This meeting exploded the myth that had developed around the teacher. Faustus was no in way the kind of wise man he was touted to be.

Augustine was disillusioned. He moved first to Rome and then to Milan and became intrigued with the Skeptics, who taught him how elusive truth really was. They claimed that there was no objective truth. Each person created his own truth. In the wake of his disappointing experiences, this seemed plausible to Augustine.

It was only through an encounter with the preaching of Ambrose, bishop of Milan, that Augustine eventually came to reappreciate the God of revelation in the Scriptures. Ambrose's preaching spoke to the deepest recesses of his soul. Augustine moved to Cassiciacum, near Lake Como, to live a more reflective life. He studied Neoplatonism with some companion philosophers.

This last plan was abandoned through a dramatic conversion experience in a garden that is described very powerfully in his *Confessions*. He sensed he heard a voice saying: "Take up and read, take up and read."[1] He opened the Scriptures at random and found this passage: "Let us live honorably in the daylight; not in carousing and drunkenness, not in sexual excess and lust, not in quarreling and jealousy. Rather, put on the Lord Jesus Christ and make no provision for the desires of the flesh" (Rom 13:13–14).

This proved to be the graced turning point in Augustine's life. Within six months, he was baptized. Deciding to return to Africa as a servant of God, he went back to Carthage in 388. In 391 he was ordained a priest; four years later, he was appointed bishop of Hippo. Then as a new bishop he decided that it was best to lay bare his soul. He wanted the people to know what he had experienced in life. He testified that he counted it a grace to be a fellow Christian with them in need of salvation, but a danger to be their bishop. So he wrote his *Confessions* for them.

The *Confessions*

Augustine did not write his *Confessions* as a biography. Rather, it was an attempt to open his heart and recount

[1] Augustine, *Confessions* VIII, 12, trans. John Ryan (New York: Doubleday Image, 1960). Subsequent quotations are from this edition and will be cited in the text.

the journey of his life over his first thirty-three years. The entire book is written as a prayer of confession to express God's goodness, his fidelity, and his initiative, as well as Augustine's own resistance before final acquiescence.

Augustine looked back upon himself as a child and recognized that he had been no pious youngster. His tendency then had been to want everything selfishly, including his mother's milk. He played ball disobediently. He cheated in games to win. He stole from the orchard when he did not need the fruit, simply as an act of vandalism. He had a tendency to want to try anything for the sake of experience.

As Augustine looked back on his adolescence, he saw the divergent tendencies within him. He recognized that he had been intellectualizing his personal problems. He had read the *Aeneid* but did not see himself in it. He had tried to solve the problem of evil by joining the Manichaeans, which eliminated for him his sense of moral guilt. He had experienced a problem with friendship, which he described as "really a desire to be enslaved" (II, 3). He did not see the dangers of the fleshly desires. He had sought out a mistress and had fathered a child. He had found a male friend with whom he shared a great deal, but who died a few years later. He had entered into a struggle to become free of the expectations of his parents and peers. His father had wanted success, but Augustine initially disliked study. Monica wanted success for God, but Augustine was not ready to say yes to God (see II, 3; III, 11–12). When Augustine looked to his peers, he found his friends wanting him to become a good orator, not a truly mature and free man (see II, 2).

It was through the ministry of Ambrose that Augustine discovered he had been attacking a faith of fantasy, not reality. Things were not what they seemed to be. It was very significant for him to meet a man like Ambrose who could speak authentically, intelligently, and directly about God. Augustine discovered he really could enter into a genuine marriage. He recognized also the importance of solitude. He recognized the significance of becoming more aware of a deeper reality in life. He saw the necessity to take personal responsibility for his own sins, even though he recognized that he was reluctant to say yes: "Give me chastity and continence, but not yet" (VIII, 7). He also came to recognize that evil inclinations could be spiritual as well as carnal, for he often disdained those who seemed less intelligent or gifted.

Most of all, Augustine recognized that true freedom is interior (see VII, 18; VIII, 12; IX, 1). He came to appreciate that the real search in life is for God. He had to accept more humbly his own humanity. He had to lean on God to rescue him from the pattern of life upon which he had embarked. His surrender to God did not come easily. He tells us:

And lo, I heard from a nearby house, a voice like that of a boy or a girl, I know not which, chanting and repeating over and over, "Take up and read. Take up and read." Instantly, with altered countenance, I began to think most intently whether children made use of any such chant in some kind of game, but I could not recall hearing it anywhere. I checked the flow of my tears and got up, for I interpreted this solely as a command given to me by God to open the book and read the first chapter I should come upon. For I had heard how Anthony had been admonished by a reading from the Gospel at which he chanced to be present, as if the words read were addressed to him: "Go, sell what you have, and give to the poor, and you shall have treasure in heaven, and come, follow me" [Mt 19:21]. And that by such a portent he was immediately converted to you.

So I hurried back to the spot where Alypius was sitting, for I had put there the volume of the apostle when I got up and left him. I snatched it up, opened it, and read in silence the chapter on which my eyes first fell: "Let us live honorably in the daylight; not in carousing and drunkenness, not in sexual excess and lust, not in quarreling and jealousy. Rather, put on the Lord Jesus Christ and make no provision for the desires of the flesh" [Rom 13:13–14]. No further wished I to read, nor was there need to do so. Instantly, in truth, at the end of this sentence, as if before a peaceful light streaming into my heart, all the dark shadows of doubt fled away. (VIII, 12)

Some Implications

Augustine's struggles revolved around freedom, the problem of evil, sexual integration, the intellectualizing of life, and the difficulty of appreciating Sacred Scripture in the right way. These struggles do not belong to Augustine alone. People experience them in every era. They reflect the fallen human condition.

The image of sin—that is, the distorted likeness of the image of God within us—is marked by the basic disorientations that Augustine and other spiritual writers have helpfully identified for us. These disorientations are sometimes called capital sins because they are the source or deeper roots of particular concrete sins. Four of these disorientations are spiritual; three are carnal.

Pride is the first and the most fundamental. It is the human arrogance that prompts us to desire to be God, not simply his image. We tend to close off the realm of the spirit as scary or uncontrollable. It prompts us to commit *the* sin against the Holy Spirit. We close him out and refuse to be enlightened by him. The richer or more powerful or more intellectually sophisticated we become, the more we are prone to it.

Envy prompts us to want to be someone else. It is rooted in a poor appreciation of our own selves. Writers today suggest that we have a *poor self-image*. Actually, envy means that we do not recognize or accept the image of God in us. It is best addressed by the development of a wholesome sense of the uniqueness of our true self found in God. It is important to come to God utterly as we are and to sense his unique and personal love for us.

Anger is expressed in hostility. It is not the feelings of anger that are wrong, but the strong expression of angry feelings in the form of inappropriate behavior against others or destructive tendencies turned in on ourselves. There is a wholesomeness in the right use of the aggressive drives. Spiritual writers suggest that where we are at any one moment in the Christian life can often be recognized by looking at the way in which the aggressive and affective drives are working together constructively for good. When, however, the aggressive drive becomes destructive, it moves us away from God.

Avarice is often expressed today in the form of a consumer mentality. A kind of greed prompts us to seek our security in having things, having status, having success, having applause. We are called in the Christian life to embrace the attitude that enables us to receive with gratitude the gifts that are made available to us in life and, then, to use them responsibly. This means using them insofar as they help us to fulfill our destiny and surrendering them to the extent that they get in the way. These are the *spiritual* capital sins.

Among the more carnal disorientations, *gluttony* is eating and drinking self-indulgently. This is opposed to promoting a healthy integration of body and spirit. Hence, there is need for an ascetical balance, not harshness. It is spiritual motivation that should guide us so that the body can become a true sacrament of the inner spirit.

Lust is the seeking or securing of sexual gratification primarily or exclusively for ourselves rather than integrating this experience into the whole person so that we can make a gift of ourselves relationally and permanently in life. Human sexuality draws us to relationship. Genital sexuality is restricted to marriage and oriented toward progeny. Chaste life and chaste love enable us to channel the sexual drive in a responsible and disciplined way.

Sloth is that apathy that leads us to self-enclosure and human comfort. It makes it more difficult or less possible to be self-giving in the work or service we are called to render in life. It can take the form of self-serving individualism in family, community, or social life. Initiative is the graced way to counter this disorientation.

Augustine made the spiritual grappling with these disorientations more credible. He admitted quite openly his human struggle with the fallen tendencies within him. He made clear the importance of allowing God eventually to take over his life. His personal testimony can reassure and encourage us.

In our own day, we face challenging phenomena: biological engineering; the use of violence to promote religious objectives; the pervasiveness of sexual misconduct within the Church and in society at large; a sometimes bitter economic struggle between the haves and the have-nots; a disproportionate consumption of this world's goods by a fraction of the world's population at the expense of those who are impoverished; a reluctance on the part of many to take responsibility for their own lives, let alone the responsibility to participate in shaping a more just and peaceful society. What we do not always recognize or address is the roots of these issues in the capital sins. A personal failure to address pride, envy, anger, avarice, gluttony, lust, or sloth can lead to tremendous harm and evil, not only to oneself but also to innocent victims. More often than not in human society, we address the symptoms of these issues rather than their roots. The Christian spiritual teaching urges us to address the roots of sin that contribute to so much sorrow in our midst.

If we truly allow God to touch the depths of our being and we sense within ourselves that deep core that is so precious to him, we will then find ourselves more ready to address those dimensions of sin that are still at work within us. The ability to identify the capital sins helps us to appreciate what may undergird concrete sins we commit in life. They reveal to us the roots of the sins in our own lives. Progress in conversion depends so much upon our being more in touch with these roots of sin and bringing them to God for healing. We cannot uproot the capital sins from our lives. We can, however, by his grace, experience a moderation of their power over us. This is a work of grace.

In the Church's spiritual tradition under the inspiration of the Holy Spirit, those who want to take seriously the Christian spiritual life have discovered the special value of bringing to the sacrament of penance and reconciliation not just serious sin but also the roots of sin within that are expressed in lesser ways in our life. This is one of the most powerful ways of exposing the depths of the disorientation within us to God's loving grace. It can help us greatly to uncover the richness of the sacramental grace God wants to offer to us on the road to deeper life.

Life, then, is a pilgrimage and a quest. The spiritual goal must become central. Augustine came to develop a profound appreciation for the need for God's grace and the special role that Christ offers to us in the Church. For him, Christ could never be separated from the Church. He wanted to help others appreciate that it is in the Church that the desire for God is nurtured, the wisdom of divine revelation offered, and the grace to live a virtuous life made more available to us. Conversion of heart opens us to receive these gifts.

Lord Jesus, how comforting it is for me to know that it is all right for me to come to you as I am. I do not have to hide from you. You want me to come with all my weakness and sinfulness to sense your more powerful love and grace. Help me to grow in confidence in coming to you with a transparent heart and soul. Take over my mind and heart and will so that I may belong more completely to you. Amen.

CHAPTER 4

Maturing in Love

Aelred on Friendship

The experience of solitude invites us to face more realistically the truth about God, ourselves, others, and the world. This leads us to address the question, How does God see us and call us? The image doctrine provides us with an inspired understanding of the way in which God has implanted his own image within us. The loss of our likeness to God necessitates real conversion of heart and life. Now it is important for us to explore how love, released in a positive direction, helps us to make genuine progress in the Christian spiritual life. For this we turn to Aelred of Rievaulx and his treatise *On Spiritual Friendship*.

Aelred of Rievaulx

Aelred lived in Scotland and then England in the twelfth century. The Viking invasions had wrought terrible suffering upon the people of the British Isles. The Church was attempting to strengthen her own life and discipline. At the end of the previous century, Pope Gregory VII, sometimes called Hildebrand, had introduced significant reform in the Church. He did his best to free the Church of royal control in episcopal appointments. He tried to promote celibacy among the clergy, even before it became a universal norm for the Western Church in 1215.

This was also a period marked by the appeal of romantic love among the young. Troubadours sang of erotic love apart from marriage. Sexual self-discipline that had marked some earlier periods yielded to a sexually promiscuous culture.

In this atmosphere, Aelred grew up in a noble family in Scotland. His father, grandfather, and great-grandfather had been married priests. His early learning came from priests. Later he was entrusted to the court of the King of Scots to receive training in nobility. While there, he was sent on a mission from the court of the King of Scots to York and stopped on his way at the Abbey of Rievaulx.

Aelred had already been troubled by the superficiality of his own existence, the lack of direction that marked his life, and the evil that he recognized coming to the fore in his service at the court of the King of Scots. His visit to the Abbey of Rievaulx awakened in him an interior desire for a more directed way of life. After completing his mission, he returned to Rievaulx and sought admission. The abbey accepted him, first as a candidate then as a professed member. He eventually became a master of novices and adviser to Abbot William of Rievaulx.

Abbot William sent Aelred on a mission to Rome. He went by way of France and spent some time with Bernard of Clairvaux. When he returned, he was appointed abbot of a new foundation in Rivesby. When William died, Aelred was elected abbot of Rievaulx, where he served from 1147 to 1167. As abbot of Rievaulx he was head of all the Cistercian monasteries in England.

Aelred became an adviser and a confidant to Pope Alexander III. He also was sought out by King David of

Scotland, King Henry II of England, and King Louis VII of France for counsel and wisdom. Dating back to his first meeting with Bernard of Clairvaux in 1142, Aelred remained a friend to Bernard and was deeply influenced by his spirituality. In fact, Aelred, because of his warm devotional spirituality and charismatic personality, was often referred to as the Bernard of the North.

Aelred wrote the *Mirror of Charity* at the request of Bernard of Clairvaux. It was developed from a series of conferences that he gave as master of novices. Aelred's treatise *On Spiritual Friendship* is his most famous work. It is modeled after the treatise on friendship by Cicero. His more philosophical treatise, *On the Soul*, is not particularly remarkable. Unfortunately, we have lost a volume of some three hundred letters written to kings, bishops, and nobles.

Aelred's Teaching on Friendship

In the first book of his treatise *On Spiritual Friendship*, Aelred addressed the nature of good Christian friendship. Christ, according to Aelred, is the bond of such friendship: "What more sublime can be said of friendship, what more true, what more profitable, than that it ought to, and is proved to, begin in Christ, continue in Christ, and be perfected in Christ?"[1]

He distinguished between charity, which he considered to have a far wider embrace, and friendship, which is for those to whom we can fearlessly entrust our hearts. He also introduced a distinction between three kinds of friendship:

[1] Aelred of Rievaulx, *On Spiritual Friendship* I, 10 (Kalamazoo, Mich.: Cistercian Publications, 1977). Subsequent quotations are from this edition and will be cited in the text. Also, see Aelred of Rievaulx, *Mirror of Charity* (London: Catholic Book Club, 1962), for his treatment of Christian sacrificial love.

carnal friendship, which constitutes a mutual harmony in the vices; *worldly friendship*, which is based upon the hope of personal gain; *spiritual friendship*, wherein there is a similarity of life, morals, and pursuits among those who truly seek what is right. Obviously, spiritual friendship is the only one that is deserving of the name Christian.

In the second book, Aelred, identifying those characteristics that indicate good Christian friendship, tells us that we should be able to experience the joy of speaking candidly of our own inner life with a genuine friend. In this relationship, nothing is feigned. The beginnings of this friendship are marked by a purity of intention, the direction of reason, restraint, and moderation. If it is truly Christian, it involves even a willingness to die for a friend (see II, 33).

Aelred was not reluctant to identify those factors that signal difficulty in friendship. An overeagerness can lead a person to be deceived and to mistake the counterfeit for the real. An aimless or puerile affection can lead to more carnal expressions of love. If friendship is rooted in the seeking of advantage for self, it can become worldly, for "no true friend leads another to the death of the soul" (II, 69).

Aelred then moved on in Book III to explore those factors that help to *preserve* good friendship. For him it was important that both persons seek the love of God above all. The expression of human love must be guided by *reason* as well as affection. He insisted that it is very important in the early stages to be discerning. He recognized that inevitably there is going to be a temporary period of testing of genuine friendship in its early stages. Genuine friendship truly leads to loyalty, right intention, discretion, and patience. Those who share this friendship should experience a profound equality, a mutual respect for one another's dignity, genuine solicitude, and a true reverence. Each should be able to correct the other in love. Aelred considered good friendship to be an *art*.

Christian Sacrificial Love

Aelred's treatise on spiritual friendship is a more specific treatment of Christian charity. In his *Mirror of Charity* and in other treatises of Cistercian origin, the Christian tradition about love is explored. Love is always operative in our lives. But Christians differentiate between two different kinds of love: the love of self-giving (*agape*) and the love of self-concern (*eros* or *cupidity*). In his *City of God*, Augustine interpreted human history in terms of a struggle between *agape* and *eros*. This ongoing struggle in the history of the human race is replicated in some way in each of our lives.

Christian sacrificial love (*agape*) is the goal of the Christian spiritual life. Because our fallen human nature inclines us to selfish love (*eros*), we need God's redemptive grace to realize it. This truly Christian love has three principal expressions: the love of the true self, an authentic love for others, and true love of God. Each of these demands a further explanation.

The *love of the true self* develops only when we experience a greater at-homeness within the self. This is rooted in a profound sense of God's personal love for us, helping us to appreciate our own movement toward good, despite the evil desires that still remain. If we experience a more peaceful conscience because we are bringing what is evil to God for forgiveness and healing, the deeper goodness in us emerges with greater confidence and strength. We sense ourselves more lovable and more free to do what is wholesome and good.

An *authentic love for others* is strengthened when the true self makes greater room for a caring presence to others.

The greatest care we can show to others is to be concerned about their eternal destiny. We need to recognize various degrees of responsibility of love for family, for those linked to us by duty, for those with whom we share friendship, for those who may be dependent in society or in need, even for those who seem to be our enemies. Obviously, we have a greater responsibility to reach out to those who have a greater claim on our love and care. This responsibility diminishes as the relationship becomes more removed. But we can never dismiss altogether the claim of those who are in need through no fault of their own. Nor can we reject those who have injured us. Harboring resentments against them will rob us of inner peace and keep us from sharing more in God's own redemptive love.

The *true love of God* is deepened by an ever-greater sense of God's love for us. As St. John has taught us: "In this is love, not that we loved God, but that he loved us and has sent his Son to be the expiation for our sins" (1 Jn 4:10). When we allow the realization of this profound prior love of God for us to touch the depths of our being, a spark is ignited within us. This spark gradually becomes fanned into a flame as we accept God's grace to make acts of love for him and of others in him. Gradually, we find ourselves released from a preoccupation with self-interest and interior conflicts that otherwise compete with him. We are enabled to move from a servile fear to a profound reverence. This love, even though often not experienced with any emotion, becomes more and more a driving force of our lives.

Attitude Toward Our Bodies

In our treatment of Christian sacrificial love, it may be helpful to focus on the distinctively Christian understanding of the human body. Christianity has always taken the body seriously, since the Son of God assumed a human body in order to become one of us. In fact, when some of the earliest heretics denied that Christ's own body was real, the Church took a very strong stand against this. The Son of God truly became fully human. Hence, the human body is holy. It is integral to the human person.

Various philosophies or theologies at work in the world have taken dramatically different positions on the origin and role of the body in life. These have not been idle theoretical discussions. The Jews believed in the goodness of the body because the body came from the creative hand of God. The Manichaeans looked upon the body as evil, since they taught that it came from an evil deity. The Platonists regarded the body as the prison for the soul.

These varying theories about the body highlight the ambiguous way in which we experience the human body. We sense its beauty, its goodness, its strength. We also experience it as enfleshing conflicting and sometimes depraving emotional drives. As a result, there has been in human history a twofold approach at work among human beings: on the one hand, a tendency to become Stoics by gaining a strong, if not rigid, control over the emotional and physical impulses; on the other hand, a tendency to become Epicureans, allowing full vent to emotional desires and feelings. Both Stoics and Epicureans fail to bring appropriate discernment between healthy and unhealthy responses to desire and feeling.

The basic Christian stance, however, is a disciplined reverence for the body. We believe that the body has been created by God. It is therefore good, even though wounded by sin. It was originally intended to form a profound unity with the soul. We have experienced a disruption of this harmony through the original fall. It is further aggravated by personal sin. The possibility of recovering this harmony is granted through the redemption offered to us in Jesus Christ. This redemption is mediated to us initially through the sacrament of baptism. This rebirth has made our bodies "temple[s] of the Holy Spirit" (1 Cor 6:19).

What has happened for us in principle in baptism becomes more a part of our human experience only as we move through the spiritual journey. Our bodies groan for the fullness of redemption (see Rom 8:22–23).

The more our bodies experience this redemption, the more they become a genuine sacrament of the inner spirit. We need to find ways to let the inner spirit shape gesture, facial expression, and embrace. A gentle but firm self-discipline enables us to express the goodness of our bodies as it harnesses the drives within them for appropriate behavior. Self-indulgence, on the other hand, becomes a form of punishment to the body. It ultimately takes its toll—physically, emotionally, and spiritually.

As Christians we are called to embrace a true bodily asceticism in order that our bodies may become a sacrament of the inner spirit. We want to open our hearts to God. We want to proclaim belief in a satisfaction that is to come. We believe in the resurrection of the body. Hence, we need to develop an appropriate approach to work, leisure, food, drink, comfort, pleasure, exercise. In a particular way we need to face the roots of carnal disorientation. Gluttony needs to yield to temperance; lust to chaste love; sloth to healthy initiative.

This ascetical approach has implications not just on a personal level but also on an environmental level as well. The disciplined but reverential approach that we take toward our bodies is intended to be extended as well to the physical environment in which we live. A respectful and disciplined use of nature makes it possible for us to enjoy a healthy, natural environment in which to live.

Human Sexuality

Obviously, sexuality impacts human life and relationships. It is important to recognize that sexuality involves much more than genital experience. It impels us toward caring human relationships. Society's current preoccupation with genital sexuality tends to distract us from this truth. For instance, we tend to use the word "sex" when we actually mean genital activity. But sexuality is far deeper and broader than genital involvement. It encompasses our affective relationships with one another.

For all Christians, there has to be a movement from lust to chaste love. We need to treat our humanity seriously and patiently. We have drives, feelings, attractions, bodily responses. We can also experience strong sexual emotions. These emotions can produce strong inclinations to genital arousal and a desire for satisfaction for its own sake.

However, if we ask God's grace and introduce gentle self-discipline, the genital urge can be transformed so that our bodies become sacraments of the inner spirit. All genital expressions should be truly a sacrament of consecrated marital love open to God's creative presence and to the total self-giving of spouses. When entered into with reverential respect and deep mutuality in affection, this expression of love becomes self-giving and uniting. Christ's teaching on sexuality in the Church is not opposed to sex but helps us discover how to channel sexual emotions and drives in a life-giving way. Any pursuit of selfish sexual pleasure, while artificially stifling the creative function, becomes a counterfeit expression of love.

Celibate love renounces all genital expression, while seeking affectionate and caring relationship on a broader and deeper level. It does not involve giving up sexuality but channeling it into chaste human relationships. For celibate love to mature, it must be accompanied by an ever more expansive concern for others. To the extent that the inner life is developed, there is a greater chance that we express ourselves bodily in a way that is truly uplifting. Chaste love brings a true inner freedom and joy.

Some Implications

A significant sign of growth in the spiritual life is the emerging sense of harmony between body and spirit. A gentle but firm asceticism allows the body truly to become a sacrament of the inner spirit and the inner spirit to manifest itself in the body. A reasonable self-discipline with regard to food, drink, exercise, rest, and relationships can bear rich fruit.

How do we treat our bodies? Do we truly befriend them? Do we try to recognize their legitimate needs for moderate, healthy food and drink? Are we able to limit ourselves when impulsive or compulsive eating or drinking tends to take over? Do we seek healthy, nourishing food, rather than food that enervates us?

In his account of the Gospel of Jesus Christ, Luke depicts the Lord Jesus as revealing some of the most significant truths about his Father and his relationship with us around a meal. This includes the final celebration of the Passover meal on the night before he died and the probable celebration of the first post-Resurrection Eucharist on the night he rose from the dead with the disciples at Emmaus. Do we incorporate into our family lives today a regular family meal wherein there is an anecdotal sharing of family history and current involvements? It is at table that we come to recognize more fully the deeper meaning of who we are with one another.

How do we approach exercise and rest? Do we make a disciplined effort to provide a moderate exercise for our bodies so that we can experience sufficient health to fulfill the responsibilities that are ours in life? Do we provide for enough rest to restore our energies so that we can continue to give of ourselves to others?

The recent clergy sexual scandal in the Church reminds us that Christian formation for chaste love is a continuing challenge. Even those who propose initially to answer God's call with a generous gift of themselves in celibate love can unfortunately lose their way and do incalculable harm to others. A gentle, persevering self-discipline accompanied by genuine growth in a loving self-gift to others makes fidelity to a celibate commitment possible. Celibate lovers need in a particular way to respect proper human boundaries in the pastoral care of others.

Fidelity in love always involves a clear identification of the concentric circles of responsibility that are ours in life. Family responsibilities, whether human or religious, take precedence over care for others. Those for whom we have responsibility in work take precedence over those in our neighborhood. Those with whom we share friendship have a greater claim on our care than those who are strangers. Those who are in pressing need around us call for our attention more than those who are not. Even our enemies cannot be excluded from the call for forgiveness, even though they do not have to become our friends.

Ultimately, love involves self-gift. It is to the extent that we give more and more of the inner self that we realize the invitation of *agape*. And this self-gift needs to include the care for the wider community and the whole environment in which we live.

Lord Jesus, help me to accept your gift of love in the depths of my own heart. You reach out to envelop me with your embrace. Allow me to let go of those desires and drives that draw me away from you. I want to belong to you in body and spirit. Take over my heart and life. Then, help me to be a sacrament of your love to others. Amen.

CHAPTER 5

A Holy Rhythm of Life

Benedict and His Rule

The regular experience of some period of solitude in our lives inevitably leads us to a more realistic encounter with ourselves, our God, other people, the world, and the devil. As we begin to grapple with these fundamental realities, we may feel overwhelmed by the question, Where do we go from here? That is an important question, for it highlights for us the significance of understanding ourselves and the human journey God has asked us to live. That is why we need to develop a clearer appreciation of ourselves as human persons created in God's image and destined for life with him forever.

But the image of glory in which we have been created and for which we have been destined has been marred by sin. We need to face this realistically and come to understand the deeper roots of the disorientations that are part of our inheritance. With that appreciation as a backdrop, it is then much more possible for us to address more realistically the call to develop the distinctive kind of love that helps us imitate the self-giving love of the Lord himself.

Movement toward a life of self-giving depends on the development of some basic habits of life to support it.

Hence, it is important for us to give explicit attention to the development of a way of life that encourages balance, depth, and a clear direction. For this we will turn for inspiration to Benedict and his Rule.

Background on Benedict

At the time that Benedict lived, the sixth century, mass movements of tribal peoples continued to invade the Roman provinces. New kingdoms began to develop in England, France, the Lowlands, Spain, southern Germany, northern Italy, and North Africa. Society was organized in rather structured tiers of social class. A few rich people in each town constituted an upper class. A larger portion of the population were plebeians: merchants, artisans, and freemen. But the vast majority were half slave and half free. They had some rights but were wedded to the land by legal fictions and were unable to improve their lot by moving into trades, the army, or Church service. There were many slaves. The moral life of the people left a great deal to be desired. There was little support for a more disciplined way of life.

The Church during this period was beginning to make significant progress in evangelization. A number of the Goths had become Christians. The Visigoths and the Lombards had infiltrated peacefully.

Yet Christianity in the West experienced the same mediocrity as had been experienced earlier in the East after the end of the early persecutions. People now lived free from external attack on their faith but had for the most part settled into a rather complacent expression of Christianity. Hence, a movement developed similar to that in the East that sought a more radical way of living the Christian life.

Athanasius, when exiled from Alexandria to Trier, shared in Rome the monastic experience of the East. Jerome had also spent time in the East to explore the life of the Eastern ascetics. John Cassian wrote the first summary of spiritual teaching for ascetics in the West. Ambrose, Augustine, and Martin of Tours experimented in the West with forms of monastic life.

St. Benedict was born in Nursia about the year 480. The only record we have of Benedict's life has been given to us by St. Gregory, writing almost fifty years after Benedict's death. It was included in Book II of his *Dialogues*. This contains a rather glorified account of Benedict's life and miracles.

Benedict came from a noble family and had a twin sister, St. Scholastica. He did his early schooling in Rome. He left home when he was about twenty years old. Apparently, he had been deeply influenced by the love of a woman, but he also was disturbed by the licentious lives of many of his peers. So he wanted to develop a way of life that would allow him to give himself more completely to God. Thus, he sought a support system that would encourage Christian living.

Benedict first became a hermit for three years. He wanted to work out a way of life that would enable him to support himself and those with whom he worked. A fledgling monastic community at Subiaco came to him and begged him to become their abbot. From this experience at Subiaco, Benedict founded a number of monasteries and schools, including Monte Casino.

Benedict developed his Rule of life in stages. Most likely the eight chapters on faults and the eleven on the Divine Office are among the oldest sections of the Rule. Some sections seem to be postscripts to his original texts, such as the section on the abbot and the qualities that should mark the abbot's role in relation to the monks. The final document emerged after a period of considerable development in monastic life.

The Teaching of Benedict's Rule

The prologue of Benedict's Rule captures its spirit. It begins with an invitation to obedience:

> Hearken, my son, to the precepts of the master and incline the ear of your heart; freely accept and faithfully fulfill the instructions of your loving Father that by the labor of obedience, you may return to him from whom you have strayed by the sloth of disobedience. To you are my words now addressed, whosoever you may be, that renouncing your own will to fight for the true King, Christ, do take up the strong and glorious weapons of obedience.[1]

Obedience of the heart and will lie at the foundation to Benedict's guidance. He urged the would-be disciple to embrace silence and a listening heart, to be courageous in resisting temptation, to be persevering, and to rely on God to provide strength in fulfilling the life. Hence, for Benedict, obedience was a condition for moving from a self-centered way of life to one that is truly open to God's will.

Benedict is usually credited with referring to prayer as *opus Dei*—the work of God. For Benedict, prayer involves work. Benedict spelled out the basic approach to prayer for the monk in his Rule. He encouraged reverence, humility, simplicity, and brevity in prayer.

---

[1] *The Rule of St. Benedict*, trans. and ed. Justin McCann, O.S.B. (London: Burns, Oates, 1960). Subsequent quotations are from this edition and will be cited in the text.

Benedict encouraged his disciples to do their work for the glory of God. He wanted prayer to permeate all their efforts at work. Rather than scheduling a special time for personal prayer, he directed the monks to set aside a time for extensive reflective reading, to participate in a contemplative praying of the Liturgy of Hours, and then to approach their physical work in a prayerful spirit. This pattern was much more possible in an agrarian culture, where work was mainly physical and regulated by the patterns of the daily climate. He wanted to help them offer their work as an act of worship. Thus, in describing the role of the member of the community who had responsibility for overseeing the work and the tools of the monastery, Benedict wrote: "Let him look upon all the utensils of the monastery and its whole property as upon the sacred vessels of the altar" (31).

Benedict had a profound respect for the role of silence. He was convinced that silence made it more possible for evil thoughts to die before leaking out in speech and poisoning human relations. He wanted speech to come from the heart so that the words would truly be repositories of God's spirit. He warned that useless talk undermines a contemplative heart. Benedict considered hospitality extended to wayfarers to be a very important expression of charity on the part of the monastic community. Thus, he wrote: "Let all guests that come be received like Christ, for he will say, 'I was a stranger and you took me in'" (53).

Because he considered pride to be the greatest obstacle to the spiritual life, Benedict gave extended treatment to the need for humility. In this portion of the Rule, Benedict focused on what he considered the central challenge of the spiritual life. He presented this teaching by outlining twelve steps or grades of advancement in the development of true humility. Later, Bernard of Clairvaux was to develop this teaching into a classical treatise on humility.[2]

Work in the Life of a Christian

If we are to appreciate more fully the teaching of Benedict, it is important for us to come to grips with the responsibility that God gives to us in our work. We all know that God originally gave a mandate to our first parents to develop the earth (see Gen 2:15). Work is an integral part of human life.

Yet, since the original fall, work has become quite toilsome (see Gen 3:17). It debilitates us. It tends to estrange us from ourselves. It tends to undermine a healthy attitude toward life and leisure. This has become even more true in recent centuries following the industrial, technological, and—now—cybernetic revolutions.

We really need to work *consciously* in order to be human. It is important that we are able to incorporate some part of our own unique minds and hearts into our work. This can be helped by participating in the shaping of the way in which we work. Incidentally, this is what underlies the Church's historical support for unions and its insistence on consultative processes in connection with Church work and life. When workers have the opportunity to participate in the shaping of conditions surrounding their work, there is greater chance of personal involvement. This, in turn, can humanize the experience of work.

We need to see work as sharing in the wisdom of God. Developing new techniques and approaches to work are

---

[2] For Bernard's treatment of humility, see Bernard of Clairvaux, *The Steps of Humility and Pride* (Kalamazoo, Mich.: Cistercian Publications, 1989).

not as important as learning to address our work in such a way that we experience ourselves as genuine partners with God in contributing to life in this world. How critical it is that we contemplate in order to appreciate the deeper meaning in our work. For instance, if we should be involved in research in physics or biology or cybernetics or genetics, it is so important that we exercise or engage in this study or develop the technology associated with it in a way that truly makes us partners with God. We will want to shun the development of techniques that fail to respect the very way in which he has created us and the world. This is what underlies the Church's teaching today about respecting the laws of nature in the world and in ourselves as we develop new ways to harness nuclear energy or reverence the natural environment or enhance human fertilization or develop gene therapies. We are called to respect nature both in the environment and in the human person.

If we want to approach work in a life-giving way, it is important to be clear on the precise freedom that is open to us. More often than not, we will not have as many choices regarding the nature of our work. We will have much more freedom over the *way* in which we work. Most of us end up securing the work that is available to us. But the real choice is in the way in which we become engaged in that work.

We should recognize that we are differentiated in life by our temperament. Introverts are inclined toward their own thoughts, feelings, and reactions; extroverts are oriented toward action and response to outside stimuli. Obviously, no one tendency is exclusively present in any one of us, even though there usually is a more pronounced emphasis in one direction or the other.

To address this, the spiritual writers reflected on the "Martha and Mary" incident recorded in Luke's Gospel (see 10:38–42). Mary sat at the feet of the Lord listening to him attentively while Martha, her sister, fretted over preparing the meal. Jesus rebuked Martha when she complained, not because she was working rather than listening, but because she was so focused on the wrong things. She had lost perspective!

Spiritual writers over the centuries have drawn attention to the truth that if we work the wrong way we will lose a contemplative attitude and become more anxious about our work. They make it clear that there is a Martha and a Mary in each of us. The goal is not only to *do* things but also to *see* their deeper insignificance. We should work with a deeper focus on the true significance of what we do.

Benedict's approach was to provide time for *seeing* so that monks would not be overwhelmed by *doing*. He also incorporated moments for holy leisure each day to restore the human spirit. In all of this, he wanted to make sure that his brothers understood the importance of accepting burdens when they were imposed, either by those who are in authority over them or by the office or responsibility that was theirs in life. The spiritual invitation is to find the prayerful and loving way of fulfilling them.

As human persons, we are invited to choose not *whether* we are going to live or work but *how* we are going to live and work. This struggle in Benedict's time led some young Christians to try to live together in a common life. Under Benedict's guidance, they faced the issues of working out the pattern of prayer, holy reading, work, and common leisure. We, too, are called to develop a pattern of life that fosters a harmony between body and soul, helps us to balance our responsibilities, and ensures that we provide space and time to give interior depth and purpose to our work and engagement.

Some Implications for Us

Progress in the Christian life and fidelity to the life of Christian holiness depend on our developing a real, even though flexible, pattern or rule of life. It can be helpful for us to review how we rise in the morning. This is a moment for us to give focus for the day. We can offer ourselves and all that we do as an expression of a gift of ourselves to God in appreciation for his gift of love to us. This posture enables us to experience the activities of the whole day as acts of worship. Nothing needs to be purely secular. The most ordinary of tasks in the kitchen or in the marketplace can be offered to God if they then are a further expression of this prayerful self-gift.

A reporter asked Mother Teresa what she was going to be doing after she had handed over the direction of the Missionaries of Charity to her successor, Sister Nirmala, and would no longer be visiting kings and presidents. Mother Teresa replied simply that it doesn't matter whether we're dealing with large issues or cleaning latrines, what matters is the degree of love with which we act.

Over time, we will find it important to incorporate into our days minimal periods of quiet time for prayerful communion with God. This will make it more possible to approach our work with a deeper appreciation of its significance. Silent pauses, however brief, can restore inner peace and a sense of purpose.

Meals can be a privileged time, especially for families. When we share meals with others, it is always important to be truly attentive to those with whom we dine. These are times for the retelling of human experiences and the developing of a common tradition. Children have the opportunity to become familiar with the history of their own parents.

We will want to incorporate into our weekly pattern of life appropriate physical exercise, social leisure, solitude, and time for hobbies. We will want to look for a way to offer explicit response to the needs of others. We will need to provide adequate sleep so that we can be rested for the following day.

In all of this, the pattern that we develop needs to be tested with the realities that impact our lives. We do not want to develop a regimented routine. It needs to be life-giving. It is asceticism of the heart that is ultimately important so that the inner drives are truly being channeled in support of self-giving sacrificial Christian love.

Lord Jesus, I bring to you all the weakness within me that tends to undermine the way I live and work. I offer myself and all that I do to you. Take it and make it a worthy offering to your Father and mine. Accept the gift of my mind, my will, and, most of all, my heart. Accept the work of my hands. Help me to think, judge, and act in conformity with the Father's will. Make possible within me what I cannot do on my own. Amen.

CHAPTER 6

Spiritual Warfare

Thomas à Kempis and *The Imitation of Christ*

The experience of solitude always brings with it an awareness that there are complex forces at work in our lives. We
become aware of the tug, both to the good and to the bad.
We have the opportunity to meet God, ourselves, others,
the world, and the demonic as they really are. A healthy
understanding of our dignity and our destiny enables us
to embark upon the spiritual journey of life with greater
confidence. Facing the need for conversion of heart and
life is very important at the beginning stages of this journey
and in the continuing stages as well. The development of a
self-giving love is the most significant way of becoming
a true disciple of the Lord. To do this faithfully, we need
to engage in a pattern of life that is supportive of this goal.

Serious engagement in the Christian spiritual life not
only necessitates a healthy rhythm but also confronts us
with our real enemies. The spiritual classics often use the
theme of pilgrimage for the spiritual journey that we travel
in life. But these same authors also are very realistic about
the fact that there is a warfare in which we need to be
engaged as well. To help us appreciate this more, we will
turn to *The Imitation of Christ,* usually attributed to Thomas
à Kempis.

The Experience of the Fourteenth Century

The fourteenth century was a period of considerable turbulence in human history. There were acerbic church-state quarrels on the continent. These became personalized in the struggle between King Philip the Fair and Pope Boniface VIII, and in the clashes of King Louis of Bavaria with Popes John XXII, Benedict XII, and Clement VI. During a notable portion of this period, there were two claimants to the papacy. At one time there were even three. For a significant period of time, the pope resided at Avignon in France. This century was also marked by the rise of nationalism, with its consequent tensions and conflicts. Wars took their human toll—so did the Black Plague.

Despite the emergence and flourishing of the universities during the thirteenth century in Oxford, Paris, Cambridge, Bologna, Padua, and Cologne, the fourteenth century experienced a period of academic decadence. The universities unfortunately became the scene of intellectual and political struggles that undermined authentic learning. Speculative thought began to become divorced from real life. Systematic theology became separated from moral and spiritual theology. This was also a period of considerable moral decline. The clergy had not been well educated and had received little or no spiritual formation. Monasteries and convents were torn by inner dissension. Pope Martin V even had to issue an interdict on the people of a whole diocese because of their refusal to accept Church authority.

In this atmosphere, a grassroots religious revival took place. Among various expressions of this revival was a movement on the Continent called *Devotio Moderna*. Gerard Groote (1340–1384) pioneered this movement after his conversion in his midthirties. He founded an association of copiers who transcribed books of devotion and then made them available to people to nourish their piety.

This association became known eventually as the Brethren of the Common Life. They took no vows. They offered prayer in common. They copied devotional literature by hand to make it available to ordinary lay Christians. Eventually, they established schools for boys. One group moved from Deventer to Windesheim and founded a monastery, forming a canonical religious community. This group adopted the Rule of the Canons Regular of St. Augustine in 1395. Eventually, eighty-two suffragan monasteries were established between 1395 and 1464.

The spirit of this movement was Christocentric, affective, interior, and renunciatory. It was committed to self-knowledge with a preference for solitude and a devotional approach both to the sacraments and to Sacred Scripture. This emphasis was in reaction to the speculative spirituality and the endless intellectual debates at the universities. The Brethren of the Common Life strongly emphasized affective piety and a personal relationship with Jesus Christ.

The Imitation of Christ

This milieu gave rise to the book known as *The Imitation of Christ*. We do not know for sure who was the author. Some suggest Jean Gerson, who was the chancellor of the University of Paris. Some conjecture that it might have been Gerard Groote, the founder of *Devotio Moderna*. Some think the author might have been Giovanni Gersen, who was a thirteenth-century Italian abbot. Most over the years have attributed it to Thomas à Kempis.

Thomas, the younger of two sons, was born in 1379 or 1380 and died in 1471. His parents were John and Gertrude

Haemerken. His older brother had entered the Brethren of the Common Life and eventually became prior of Mount St. Agnes at Agnetenberg, one of the monasteries of the *Devotio Moderna*. Thomas entered his brother's monastery in 1406 or 1407 and was ordained a priest in 1413. Twelve years later, Thomas became subprior and instructor of novices. He died at Mount St. Agnes in 1471. In keeping with the humble spirit of the *Devotio Moderna*, he kept hidden most of the details of his life.

The author of the spiritual doctrine contained in *The Imitation of Christ* took the renunciation passages in Sacred Scripture very seriously. He encouraged the development of a personal following of the Lord. He recommended a simple piety in the face of a culture and society that seemed to be crumbling around him. The spirit of the book is captured in its first chapter:

> The highest wisdom is this: to aim for the heavenly kingdom through indifference to the world. Vanity it is, therefore, to strive for perishable riches and to rely on them. Vanity, too, it is to court honors and to set oneself up for lofty estate. Vanity it is to go after fleshly desires and long for that by which you must be heavily punished. Vanity it is to wish for a long life and care little about a good life. Vanity it is to attend only to the life that is and not foresee the days that are ahead. Vanity it is to love what is passing at full speed and not hasten there where lasting joy awaits.[1]

A fundamental principle underlying the teaching of *The Imitation of Christ* is, all that God has created is good, but

---

[1] Thomas à Kempis, *Imitation of Christ* I, 1, trans. Edgar Daplyn (New York: Sheed and Ward, 1952). Subsequent quotations are from this edition and will be cited in the text. For *The Imitation of Christ*'s attitude toward the world, see Charles Healey, "The Imitation of Christ Revisited", *Review for Religious* 36 (1977): 551–56.

we should renounce those persons and things that do not help us to fulfill the very purpose for which they have been created. Hence, we need to judge carefully how to use the creatures God gives us in life.

For the author of *The Imitation*, charity is more important than any great deed. Without love, he tells us, external life produces nothing; but whatever is done for love, however small and contemptible, becomes holy, fruitful. For God considers more the purpose with which you work than the actual work done. He does much who loves much. He does much who does a thing well. He does well who serves the community rather than his own choice (see I, 15).

Thomas à Kempis identified the root of much of our restlessness in the untamed drives and desires within us: "Whenever a man has an unruly longing for anything, he is at once restless within himself. The proud and the covetous never rest; the poor and lowly of spirit are kept in abounding peace" (I, 6).

The author was also suspicious of the seeking of one's own will:

> Therefore do not be too settled in your own opinion, but cheerfully be willing to listen to the ideas of others. If your idea is good, but you give it up for God, and follow another, you may gain the more for that. For I have often heard that it is safer to hear and accept advice than to give it. It may also come about that each one's thought may be good, but to refuse to agree with others when reason or the case itself demands it, is a sign of pride and obstinacy. (I, 9)

When we *do* sinfully seek our own will, contrition is then very important. As the author said: "I would rather feel compunction than know its definition" (I, 1).

Thomas à Kempis was very realistic about the struggle we have to address in order to be faithful to the Gospel in our lives. He taught that, in fidelity to the Christian spiritual tradition, we are engaged in genuine spiritual warfare in the living out of Christian life. In addressing this warfare, he maintained it is important not to be afraid of adversity. He exhorts us to be on guard against complacency, to be wary of unlimited human interchange, to direct our efforts toward the struggle for virtue.

Following the invention of the printing press, *The Imitation of Christ* became the most published book after the Bible itself. The piety within it touched the heart of the ordinary person. Although this piety was not always sufficiently related to doctrine, the author never intended it to express a theologically complete treatise. It was always intended to be a book that moved the heart. Readers would just take short passages and meditate on them.

The Imitation seems to encourage a withdrawal from the world and a skeptical attitude toward ourselves and the world. It should be read as if it were talking about the world that is not yet fully redeemed and the self that is not yet fully sanctified. We need to be wholesomely skeptical about them so that the truly redeemed world and the truly saved self might emerge more fully.

There is a strong emphasis on the interior life and the relationship between the individual and God. If this is understood in an exclusive sense, not including relationships with others, it obviously constitutes a problem. This, however, is not the intention of the author. The book is intended to be read in short passages and to inspire disciples to live the Christian life more spiritually and faithfully.

Holy Warfare

There are times when each of us has the experience of being overwhelmed by the powers of evil in the world. This is particularly true when we experience the escalating violence that devastates us today. Domestic violence, violence in our streets and schools, and acts of terrorism unsettle us tremendously. When we experience this, we know that we are engaged in a real war. It is not a political or military war.

The struggle that we face is a struggle between God and the demonic for the soul of the human person. It is a struggle for the right kind of love: the love of self-sacrifice and charity rather than that of self-regard and cupidity. The aggressive drives within us should be focused on struggling against the forces of evil. They need to be disciplined for this purpose. To the extent that the affective and aggressive drives within us are working together in service to love, we will develop courage, patience, perseverance, and fortitude. But the demands of the *Martha* within us can become so great that they obscure or snuff out the life of the spirit. In Luke's account, Martha was rebuked for losing perspective. We need to assume our responsibilities generously but also see the realization of salvation as the most important reality in all of life.

Origen, one of the greatest Church Fathers, taught that the battleground in life is ultimately in the human heart. We experience conflicting desires and drives tugging at the heart. We need to discern between those that we want to act on and those we want to let die.

Silence and solitude provide us with the opportunity to recognize the significance of this battle and to harness the inner energy to cooperate with God's grace in making the right choices. The movements within us flow from both the redeemed and unredeemed portions of our nature. We want to nurture the first; we want to resist the latter. Hence, two fundamental truths guide the Christian life: the life of grace truly builds on nature; but we need to embrace the cross to discipline that portion of our nature not yet fully redeemed. This cross is never embraced without a struggle.

Living the Christian life requires authentic discretion. There has to be some separation between our own lives and the life of the world. Otherwise we simply make peace with the fallen world. We need to become athletes, fighting against the demonic and for God. We must find a simple and real relationship with God. God alone suffices in life.

Let us make no mistake. The demonic is real. We are in frequent encounters with the powers of evil. We experience some evil forces at work in our closest relationships, in community, in churches, in our nation. How often do we meet people who are in themselves good, yet seem to be to a greater or lesser extent under the power of evil!

We need to acknowledge the existence of the devil while not exaggerating his power. He is in competition with God. Spiritual reality is both good and bad. But Christ has won a definitive victory over him. It is ours to participate in Jesus' victory.

If we do not acknowledge the existence of the demonic, we will often end up struggling against other people instead. We may even demonize them. However, we need to remember that people are not evil in themselves. They may be more or less under the influence of the devil and then do very evil things. Imitating and sharing in the approach of the Lord Jesus, we are to seek to free others from the power of the devil by the way in which we love what is deepest in them and help them to resist the power of evil that may be at work within them. This is why we are called to hate the sin but to love the sinner.

Unfortunately, in our fallen human condition we have a tendency either to deny the existence of the devil or to exaggerate his power. When we deny his existence, we give up the struggle to resist the powers of evil within ourselves and within others. If we exaggerate his existence, we can focus on the more overstated and extraordinary ways in which the devil can manifest himself—as some recent literature or films or television programs have. The teaching and celebration of the sacraments of baptism, penance, and anointing of the sick help us to focus in a balanced way on the reality and the influence of the devil. We encounter the Lord Jesus in each of these sacraments and enlist his power and grace to win a victory over the devil. Ultimately, it is God's victory in Christ Jesus that makes it possible for us to be victorious as well.

Some Implications for Us

The reality of this spiritual struggle in the living of the Christian spiritual life has profound implications for our coming to grips with our aggression—one of the more troubling strong drives at work within us. Our aggression can be a powerful force for good or can lead to terrible destruction. Considerable confusion seems to exist about the best way to harness the aggressive drive in service to what is good.[2]

We become particularly conscious of the aggressive drive when we experience anger. In itself anger is neutral— a reaction to threat, hurt, danger, or frustration. The question, however, for us as Christians is this: Is our anger becoming a stumbling block or a stepping-stone to deeper life? To answer it, let us consider the sources of our anger.

A common source of frustration and anger is the very limitedness, or finiteness, of our human existence. Part of

[2] For a discussion of anger, see Alfred Hughes, "Anger: Stumbling-block or Stepping-stone to Graced Originality", *Studies in Formative Spirituality* 1 (1980): 93–102.

us would like to be God; it resents any and all experience of human limitation. In reality, however, we are very finite human creatures. We can do nothing to change some of the basic realities in our life: our physical birth, our life history, the finite nature of our intellect, our emotional and spiritual abilities, and the inevitability of our death. There are many givens in our life, including innumerable circumstances that limit the very real possibilities for us. This experience of finiteness frustrates an inner craving for omnipotence. This frustration can lead to festering anger. Any desire within us that is unchecked seeks ever-greater satisfaction and then experiences frustration when that satisfaction cannot be realized. We then tend to consider life unfair. We may even blame God himself because he is the Author of life.

A second source of our anger may be our own personal sin. Beyond the natural limitations of finite human existence, we can introduce even more suffering into our lives by sinful decisions and sinful patterns of life. This takes on a particularly virulent form when we become addicted to pleasure, artificial stimulants, work, or the compulsive pursuit of any illusory satisfaction. The human urge for satisfaction drives us on, while the experienced gratification diminishes. We become consumed by a craving that cannot be quieted. We become impatient with ourselves and then often direct this impatience at others.

A third source of our anger may be the sin of others. We are born into the sinful situation. Despite the basic goodness of this world and all human life, something has gone unmistakably wrong. We are heirs to this at birth. We continue to suffer the consequences of the sins of others as we pass through life. Deceit and violence permeate life in a very frightening way. There is no one who is free from the impact of the sins of others. Unrestrained anger can incline us to do violence to others in retaliation.

Finally, we can also recognize a fourth possible source for our suffering and therefore consequent anger: the purifying love of God. Without oversimplifying ways in which God enters human life, we can be certain that he sometimes allows and may even want to purify us directly by the very suffering he asks us to experience. In some way, this is also true of all the suffering we undergo.

Authentic Christian spirituality invites us to build on a wholesome respect for the truly human. The aggressive drive within us is integral to sound humanity. The road to Christian holiness cannot invite us to trample underfoot the capacity for strong action. In fact, it is the aggressive drive that enables us to express courage and fidelity in the midst of hardship and resistance to evil in every form. If we realize this, then we can begin to explore creative ways to draw on God's grace in transforming any destructive tendencies into virtuous behavior. The battleground is in the heart. The question is, Are we going to be more inwardly open to God's Holy Spirit or to the devil?

One source of our anger is the experience of human limitation. We are not dealing here with moral evil. We are facing the very real aggravation that comes from being finite. God has given to us a graced nature. He has granted special gifts to us that he wants us to develop (see Mt 25:14–29). He has also asked us to recognize that the egotistical self can take over in life unless we are willing to renounce it (see Lk 14:26–27). We are, then, called to recognize that what we are and what we have are fundamentally gifts from God. We are to receive them with thanksgiving and return them gratefully to God in the way we use them in fulfillment of his loving purposes for others. We are to live not only graciously and with dignity but also within our limitations. We do not have unlimited control over our lives. There is a prayer in the Christian spiritual tradition that helps us to develop the appropriate dispositions of mind and heart: "God grant me the serenity to accept the things I cannot change, the courage to change the things I can, and the wisdom to know the difference."

In recent decades, this prayer, attributed to Reinhold Niebuhr and called the Serenity Prayer, has been taken over by the twelve-step programs to help people move beyond addiction.

A second source of our anger is our personal sin. This may be more difficult for us to cope with because we experience such ambivalent feelings about guilt. Initially, the acknowledgment of guilt seems to be very demeaning. We associate feelings of shame with it and want to run from this kind of humiliation. We indulge in self-justification. There is no doubt but that our own sin introduces real suffering into life and contributes to a festering anger. As Augustine has revealed to us in his *Confessions*, the tortuous journey of running away from our guilt is going to only increase our suffering. Eventually, we need to come to God with a repentant heart. Confession, then, has less to do with shameful self-revelation and far more to do with opening the depths of our souls to God's healing love calling us to our unique goodness beyond the enslaving power of sin.

There is no question but that the sin of others brings considerable suffering into our lives. It is indeed a great source of frustration and can easily lead to anger. This has become in our own society a very prevalent phenomenon. The violent acts of others and political or economic systems that reinforce sinful structures of life can wreak havoc. Who of us still living will ever forget the traumatic attacks of September 11, 2001?

A legitimate object for our anger, even our hatred, is the sinful evil and the Evil One. This Evil One is the author of deceit and violence about whom the Lord Jesus has warned us (see Jn 8:44). If we focus our anger on the evil itself and the demonic as the ultimate author of that evil, then we are going to be less apt to look for a convenient scapegoat for our anger and unjustly condemn fellow human beings. If we fail to make this distinction, we will inevitably focus our anger on specific people. Actually, it is only in seeing the real beauty and nobility in others and then wanting to free one another from the destructive power of the Evil One that we truly participate in the diminishment of evil. This is what Jesus did on the Cross: "Father, forgive them; for they know not what they do" (Lk 23:34).

Innocent though he was, Jesus bore the full brunt of the accumulated moral evil in the world. In the image of the suffering servant, he absorbed the horrendous impact of this evil and refused to retaliate in like manner (see Is 52 and 53). Jesus saw the hidden nobility in us all and was able to convert his anger into calm self-possession in the face of humiliating torture and then offer us forgiveness when he was unjustly nailed to the Cross. The inner resources, which could have legitimately led to angry rebellion, were enlisted instead in the service of redemptive love. It takes great power and strength to reverse the virulence of sin.

This teaching challenges us as we assess in the light of the Gospel our response to terrorist attacks or heinous crimes committed against us. It is appropriate for us to protect innocent people with every means available to us, to exact punishment for the serious violation of the social order, and to neutralize the possibility of such people harming innocent people again. But we must also do this, not in a spirit of revenge but out of redemptive desire ultimately to lead the perpetrators to conversion of heart and life.

Finally, if the root of our suffering is God's purifying love, then it is ours to recognize that there is a mystery here. We should not speak too easily of God's desiring any particular human suffering. Most suffering can be traced directly to one of the more evident causes mentioned above. But, in another sense, God does allow all suffering to take place for a greater good (see Rom 8:35–39). What is important in the face of this kind of suffering is transforming any resistance welling up within us to the inner power of yielding. This yielding demands strength. It is not a passive giving up, but an active wanting what God wants: "Not my will, but yours, be done" (Lk 22:42). Only in this context can we adequately appreciate the scriptural words so often misunderstood: "The Lord disciplines him whom he loves" (Heb 12:6).

There is nothing more attractive than to experience strong sacrificial love. The reason the Church venerates martyrs is the witness they gave to their capacity to continue to love faithfully, even in the face of unjust torture and death.

Lord Jesus, you revealed to me the depth and breadth of your love in your broken heart on the Cross. You absorbed the full virulence of my sins and the sins of every person who has walked this earth. Thank you for continuing to focus on the deeper goodness within me. Thank you for restraining the hand of punishment and replacing it with the outstretched hands of forgiveness. Help me to accept even more fully your redemptive love and then to offer redemptive love to others in your name. Help me to live with courage and fidelity in the midst of human weakness that one day I may share in your total victory. Amen.

CHAPTER 7

The Goal of Prayer

Guigo's Ladder

The message from the desert is a call to introduce regular solitude in our lives so that we might come to recognize more clearly and truly who God is, who we are, who others are, what the world is, and the reality of the demonic. We tried to clarify God's view of us—creatures whom he has created with such a special destiny. Walter Hilton helped us to appreciate the fact that we are made in the image of God. We asked Augustine to help us appreciate the extent to which the likeness has been lost but can be recovered in Jesus Christ.

Having addressed then the need for conversion of heart and life, we turned to the positive development of the life of self-giving love with the help of Aelred of Rievaulx. Benedict gave us insights into the need to express this positive development in a pattern of life that supports virtuous response. *The Imitation of Christ* then brought us face-to-face with the depth and extent of the struggle in which we are engaged. This background may now allow us to turn more explicitly back to our engagement with God in prayer as we look to Guigo the Carthusian for guidance.

Guigo and His Times

Guigo lived and died in the twelfth century in what is modern-day France. The reform efforts of Pope Gregory VII, who had lived at the end of the eleventh century, continued to bear fruit on the local scenes. The Church attempted to strengthen the moral life and discipline not only of the clergy and religious but also of the lay faithful. The freeing of episcopal appointments from the control of local kings helped to diminish the possibility of a choice of bishops more for political than for spiritual reasons. The celibacy of the clergy was encouraged more and more, even though it had not yet become universally decreed in the Latin Church.

A practice had emerged in the Church of charging extra for the purchase of religious articles after they were blessed. It was called simony. The reform decrees of Pope Gregory declared that any object, even though previously blessed, would lose its blessing if it were sold. From that time on, it has been forbidden in the Church to traffic in blessed objects. They are to be blessed only after they have been purchased.

As we saw in our discussion of Aelred of Rievaulx, this century experienced a romantic revival. Troubadours sang of romantic love apart from marriage. Sexual love was acted out frequently in a way similar to our own day. So the Church in her teaching on sexuality had to assume a countercultural stance.

This was the atmosphere in which Guigo grew up in southern France. We know very little about him except that he entered the Carthusians, became the ninth prior of La Grande Chartreuse, and finally became the general of the order in 1173. He resigned that office in 1180.

The Carthusian order promoted eremitical life. But there was also a limited commitment to a common life by virtue of a shared rule. This rule regulated the personal life of each of the hermits and weekly gathering for Eucharist and a common meal.

Guigo, who died in 1188, left manuscripts behind that eventually became circulated to others. One was entitled the *Ladder of Monks*. A second was called *Meditations*.

Guigo's Teaching on Prayer

Guigo identified four rungs of prayer in his *Ladder of Monks*, which is known today as *lectio divina*. He stated them succinctly in Part II:

> *Reading* is the careful study of the Scriptures, concentrating all one's powers on it. *Meditation* is the busy application of the mind to seek the help of one's own reason for knowledge of hidden truth. *Prayer* is the heart's devoted turning to God to drive away evil and obtain what is good. *Contemplation* is when the mind is in some sort lifted up to God and held above itself, so that it tastes the joys of everlasting sweetness.[1]

In subsequent sections of his treatise, Guigo then explained what he meant by each of these. Let us address each of them separately.

For Guigo, *reading* involves picking up the Scriptures, invoking the light of the Holy Spirit, and then reading them as slowly and thoughtfully as possible. He described it as taking solid food in the mouth. It involves wanting to let the words of Scripture sink in or be ingested so that they can nourish the whole person. Thus, the careful reading of Scripture becomes the primary source for prayer.

[1] *Guigo II: Ladder of Monks and Twelve Meditations*, trans. Edmund Colledge, O.S.A., and James Walsh, S.J. (Kalamazoo, Mich.: Cistercian Publications, 1997). Subsequent quotations are from this edition and will be cited in the text.

Meditation then becomes the studious involvement of the mind, probing a deeper understanding of the hidden truth. He described this as chewing the food that has been ingested in the mouth. He also used the image of digging for a treasure. He described the application of the intellect enlightened by faith as seeking understanding. The result of this effort was to be an increased understanding of the blessed life that we are called to live.

Prayer is the devout turning of the heart to God. Guigo referred to this as seeking the flavor of the food. Having identified the desired treasure, we are to ask that we might be given it. We beg for the grace to be able to live the life that is now a little more profoundly understood. *Prayer* expresses the personal realization that we cannot move from understanding to action without God's grace. Living the life that is presented in Sacred Scripture is possible only by the mercy of God.

Contemplation then becomes the movement of the mind beyond ourselves. Guigo described this as enjoying the nourishment of the food. It involves experiencing the fruit of prayer. By God's grace we begin to sense from within the life that God invites us to live.

According to Guigo, beginners in prayer will have to focus more time on *reading*. Those more experienced will focus more on meditation. The further along we move, less reading will make possible more *meditation*. Then we will need less *meditation* to move us to more *prayer*. Finally, we will need to dwell less with *prayer* before moving into increased *contemplation*. But Guigo insists that these movements should come about in a human fashion. It is inevitable that the experience of God in prayer is going to fluctuate. We will need to move back and forth, depending upon what else is going on in our lives. But as Augustine made clear, the person who truly desires God already begins to possess him. Perhaps it would be better expressed by saying that God already possesses us more fully when we truly desire him.

Reading

Holy reading has always been considered very important for the spiritual life. We need to be nourished by God's word as expressed in an inspired fashion in Holy Scripture and then as interpreted and lived within the Church. Unfortunately, as prayer has become more divorced from reading, study, and reflection, the significance of holy reading has come to be underemphasized. But the desert pioneers, as well as Augustine, Jerome, Isidore, and others, focused principally on reading as the nourishment for prayer. Benedict's Rule scheduled time for reading and presumed prayer would happen in connection with that. Prayer was to be a lifting of the mind and heart in the course of reading and then to be carried on throughout the day during the physical work in which the monk was to be engaged. Aelred criticized the failure to incorporate reading into religious life.

Guigo described the life of a solitary as the life of good reading. In the course of the history of the Church, reading was, unfortunately, gradually reduced to instruction on how to help people to be pious rather than bringing them into contact with the life-giving truths of salvation. We cannot persevere in the Christian life without due attention to holy reading.

Meditation

The original meaning of meditation was *rehearsal*. It referred to the oral repetition of the text in order to ponder it more completely and then to memorize it and internalize it. Hugh of St. Victor treated meditation as a reflection on creation, Sacred Scripture, and the moral life. Guigo was in the reading/meditation tradition but treated meditation in a more reflective way. Aelred considered reading to be an ordinary part of life and meditation the way to nurture spiritual affection.

The postmedieval use of fantasy in meditation began to separate meditation from the reading of the sacred texts. Later, in the sixteenth century, Ignatius of Loyola reintroduced this discipline by returning the disciple to the text. He recommended the use of the imagination to illustrate the text while bringing both an intellectual pondering and an affective response to the prayer.

Other post-Tridentine reformers such as St. Francis de Sales, St. Teresa of Ávila, St. Vincent de Paul, and Pierre Cardinal de Bérulle proposed concrete approaches to meditative prayer as a way to assist the serious disciple to incorporate the teaching of the spiritual tradition into daily life.

Prayer

As we have seen, meditation for Guigo involved ruminating on the sacred texts to seek understanding. Prayer, according to Guigo, leads us to the petitioning for the grace to live the graced insights resulting from meditation. For Hugh of St. Victor, meditation is the mind's attempt to discover the truth; prayer is the mind's lively penetration of the truth. For Gregory the Great, prayer is desire to pray whether the petition is fully articulated or not. William of St. Thierry described prayer as the affection of the Christian cleaving to God.

Thomas Aquinas treated prayer as a matter of intention. It is expressive of the desire even if the mind wanders. He called it a good work and expected that spiritual refreshment would come from it.

St. Teresa of Ávila identified attention as the key to prayer. She did not make an essential distinction between meditation, mental prayer, and good vocal prayer. For her, it is attention that introduces the conditions for more affective engagement with the pondering of the text and response to God's word. As we have seen above, Guigo considered the intellect to be more involved in meditation, the heart more involved in prayer.

Contemplation

Guigo taught that contemplation culminated the life of prayer. It involves direct experience of God, in which the inner senses come alive through special grace.

Gregory the Great differentiated between what he called *the active life* and *the contemplative life.* The active life is constituted by acts of charity. The contemplative life is marked by the love of God and neighbor without the necessity of external activities. Although Gregory never suggested that anyone is called exclusively to one kind of life, he distinguished among Christian disciples in accordance with their call. People are called more to one or to the other. But he wanted people in either vocation in life to be faithful to the inner contemplative call.

Thomas Aquinas placed a great deal of emphasis on the involvement of the deeper recesses of the mind in contemplative prayer. Meister Eckhart promoted contemplation as a way to deeper and more fruitful activity in life. James of Milan described contemplation as leading to deeper compunction of heart and the desire to avoid any approach to life that may offend God. He encouraged a constant affective union with the Passion of the Lord. He considered contemplation as strengthening the determination to desire nothing but God.

In the sixteenth century, Ignatius of Loyola went to great lengths to integrate contemplation with action. Teresa of Ávila and John of the Cross considered meditation to be an attentive pondering of the truth of salvation, while contemplation was to be the experience of being drawn beyond our human capacities in prayer. The spiritual tradition consistently identified contemplation with a more interior, intuitive, experiential, and grace-initiated engagement with God.

Implications for Us

The teaching on prayer contained not only in Guigo but also in the lives of those who provide a continuing witness to the spiritual tradition urges us to recognize the inseparable link between prayer and the rest of our lives. We have postponed our treatment of prayer to this point in order to ensure that we recognize that there is a whole way of life to which we need to be introduced in order for prayer to be well-grounded in authentic living. Thus, we have focused on prayer only after treating the previous dimensions of Christian living that recognize the need for true conversion of life and heart and the development of an authentic way of loving and working with realism in the struggle against the demonic. Any approach to prayer that is unrelated to the rest of life becomes unreal.

Prayer promotes communion with God. It has much more to do with communion than communication. Prayer involves fidelity in accepting the call of the inner Spirit. Prayer is intended to lead to the most profound acts of love: moments when the mystery of God and the mystery of the human person meet in the core of our being.

The enduring consciousness of God that comes from prayer is intended to permeate all that we do. Thus, prayer is rooted in our deepening appreciation of the fact that we are sacramentally incorporated into the life of the Son, calling God our Father through the power of the Holy Spirit dwelling within us. Moreover, prayer is profoundly Trinitarian and deeply sacramental.

There is no possibility of entering into deeper prayer unless we become interiorly quiet and attentive, adopting the attitude of a good listener. The wise person will keep silence until the right moment. Words are intended to reveal the inner heart. They are either the repositories of the spirit or express the corruption of sin, both original and personal. Thus, there is a need to hear the word of God in order to sense what words are then to be spoken.

In this connection Anne Lindbergh has a telling message to communicate in her book *Gift from the Sea*:

As far as the search for solitude is concerned, we live in a negative atmosphere as invisible, as all pervasive, and as enervating as high humidity in an August afternoon. The world today does not understand in either man or woman, the need to be alone. How inexplicable it seems. Anything else will be accepted by a better excuse. If one sets aside time for a business appointment, a trip to the hairdresser, a social engagement, or a shopping expedition, that time is accepted as inviolable. But, if one says: I cannot come because it is my hour to be alone, one is considered rude, egotistical or strange. What a commentary on our civilization, when being alone is considered suspect; when one has to apologize for it, make excuses, hide the fact that one practices solitude, like a secret vice. Actually these are among the most important times in one's life—when

one is alone. Certain springs are tapped only when we
are alone. The artist knows he must be alone to create;
the writer to work out his own thoughts; the musician to
compose; the saint to pray.[2]

Solitude and silence are not ends in themselves. They
are intended to nurture an at-homeness within ourselves
so that there will be room for God and for others. There is
much more involved than simple physical silence. Guigo,
at the end of his treatise, treats of four obstacles to making progress in prayer: "unavoidable necessity, the good
works of the active life, human frailty, or worldly follies".
He then goes on to say: "The first can be excused, the
second endured, the third invites compassion, the fourth
blame" (XV).

Obviously, when necessity arises there is nothing that
we can do to preserve the solitude. The good works of an
active life, if they are responsibilities of ours, are obviously
unavoidable necessities; if they are important things to do,
we can endure them. However, we should not yield to
them all the time because as Guigo said: "When we fail
to preserve the solitude and silence because of human
weakness then we need compassion" (XV).

The fourth, however, is the one for which we must
repent. If we are guilty of not preserving sufficient silence
in our lives because of our engagement in worldly follies,
then we have ourselves to blame. This is an issue that we
need to address humbly and sincerely in our own culture
that surrounds us with superficial messages and noise.

Often, when we move into this silence, we find that our
minds seem to be hyperactive on the one hand or totally
passive on the other. If the mind becomes hyperactive, the

[2] Anne Lindbergh, *Gift from the Sea* (New York: Random House, 1991), 44.

problem that St. Gregory the Great pointed out is less the thoughts than the compulsive drives that keep them going. There is a need for us to still the inner and outer voices in order to find a deeper silence. Hence, we should bring to God what wells up within us and pay particular attention to the drives that give rise to the thoughts. We need God's grace to begin to deal with them and quiet them. If we experience anxiety or fear or attachments or confusion, we need to bring that to God as well. As we persevere in placing ourselves in his hands, it will become more possible for us to become quiet and attentive.

Catherine de Hueck Dougherty, founder of Canada's Madonna House, has indicated that the real purpose of silence is inner attentiveness to reality so that we can face the facts of our own inner situation as well as the realities of God, others, the world, and the demonic:

> Hand in hand with solitude goes silence.... To be silent you have to be re-collected. That means you have to gather yourself up for we are all fragmented, you and I. Today man is fragmented. He doesn't know himself and he doesn't know his neighbor, and what is more, he doesn't care.... What does it mean to be re-collected? It means to become whole. Silence dwells in a person that is becoming whole. The deeper the wholeness the deeper the silence.... Silence is the highest form of communication and we desire to communicate passionately with one another and with God and silence is that form of communication.[3]

William McNamara has called the contemplation that is possible through silence "a long, loving look at the real".[4]

---

[3] Catherine de Hueck Dougherty, *Spiritual Reading*, August 10, 1974.

[4] William McNamara as quoted by Walter Burghardt, "Contemplation: A Long Loving Look at the Real", in *An Ignatian Spirituality Reader*, ed. George W. Traub (Chicago: Loyola Press, 2008), 91.

The Goal of Prayer

The purpose of prayer is best seen in the prayer that Jesus himself taught us. A number of the great spiritual writers in our own Christian history, beginning with Origen, treated the Our Father as the best way to teach prayer.

The purpose of Jesus' teaching was not to encourage us to keep repeating the prayer mindlessly, but to help us recognize that in that prayer are expressed the most important inner dispositions of the human heart.

Thus, as we address God as our Father we are explicitly acknowledging that in Jesus Christ we are sons and daughters of the Father and that our relationship with him is one that is shared. That is why we use *our* rather than *my*. We recognize and affirm who God is in our lives by praying that his name may be hallowed. We express the desire for salvation and sanctification, both personal and communal, as we pray that his kingdom may come. We seek to be united with Jesus in his loving sacrificial response to the Father for the sake of the mission that the Father had given to him in the world when we pray: "Your will be done on earth as it is in heaven."

As we pray for our daily bread, we express the need for our basic sustenance, both physical and spiritual. In order to make our own the prayer for forgiveness, we express our intention to make possible forgiveness for others: "Forgive us our trespasses as we forgive those who trespass against us." Hence, our refusal to forgive others means that we are not really accepting God's forgiveness and therefore cannot rightly lay claim to it.

The final petitions, asking that we may not be led into temptation and may be delivered from evil, articulate realism about the struggle with the demonic and the challenge of temptation. We need God's grace in order to be triumphant. Our ultimate prayer is that in Christ Jesus we might be freed from the Evil One. It is obvious then that prayer is profoundly related to the rest of human life.

Our Father, who art in heaven, hallowed be thy name. Thy kingdom come. Thy will be done on earth as it is in heaven. Give us this day our daily bread and forgive us our trespasses as we forgive those who trespass against us. And lead us not into temptation, but deliver us from evil. Amen.

CHAPTER 8

Prayer and Real Life

Teresa of Ávila and *The Way of Perfection*

As we address the place of prayer in our lives and the approach that the Christian spiritual tradition encourages us to follow, we recognize that our prayer, if it is to be truly Christian, needs to be rooted in God's word. Approaches to prayer, sometimes encouraged and recommended today, often seek a kind of quiet that is more psychological than spiritual. For instance, approaches to prayer that owe a great deal to the non-Christian East move us toward a self-emptying quiet. This can be a helpful first stage in prayer, but it is not at the heart of Christian prayer. Our self-emptying is intended to be a preparation for the reception of God's word and then response to him.

Sometimes approaches to prayer encouraged today move us in a much more devotional direction. Repetition of devotional prayer and the bringing to God of multiple petitions in our lives become the expression of our faith. This, too, can be helpful as a preparation for prayer. If we then place all of our petitions and, even more importantly, ourselves in God's hands, we become quietly receptive to God's word and God's enlightenment. We cannot come to our God really open to him unless we are truly bringing to him what is going on in our hearts and in our lives.

The greatest danger in the life of prayer is to give up trying to relate prayer authentically to the rest of our lives. Perhaps better expressed, we find our greatest challenge in letting prayer be an expression of the real self encountering God and dealing with the realities of our human life humbly and sincerely. For help in doing this, let us turn to Teresa of Ávila.

Teresa's Life and Times

Teresa's life spanned a good bit of the sixteenth century. She was born in 1515 and died in 1582. This was the century of the Renaissance and the Reformation. It was obvious that an old order was breaking down and a new one being born. We were later to call this the beginning of the modern period with its focus more on the human person than on God, on this world rather than the next.

People had become significantly disenchanted with the way in which the Church was living the Gospel message in the world. There had been an increasing deterioration of moral and spiritual life, especially during the previous century.

In the generation before Teresa, Martin Luther and John Calvin had begun first to institute reform within the Church and then found themselves separated from the Church of Rome. This Protestant Reformation was situated primarily in France, Germany, and Switzerland. The Iberian Peninsula, including Spain and Portugal, was largely isolated from these developments.

In Spain, however, there was a climate of intense religious revival. There were various mystical groups under the leadership of people like Francisco de Osuna and Laredo. Some of them were called Alumbrados because of the way in which they claimed to be specially enlightened by the light of the Holy Spirit. The Church of Rome instituted the Inquisition to investigate these movements. It was an effort to promote orthodoxy in teaching and in the expression of spiritual life. It also sought to identify and ferret out distortions in both teaching and devotional life.

When Teresa was thirteen years old, her mother died. Her father, after trying to offer some guidance and formation on his own, finally decided to send her to a convent school for training with the Augustinians. She became inspired by the life of the Augustinian nuns and expressed a desire to her father to become a nun. Her father felt she was too young and discouraged her.

Teresa waited until she was twenty years of age—the age of majority for young people in Spain. She left home unannounced to join not the Augustinians but the Carmelite Monastery of the Incarnation at Ávila.

In her first years at this monastery, Teresa became quite ill. In the midst of this illness, she experienced what she described as a miraculous healing. This was to have a dramatic impact upon her as she sensed that God had rescued her for a very special mission.

It can be helpful to distinguish in the life of Teresa three distinct periods in her spiritual journey. From her birth until she went to school with the Augustinians, Teresa had grown up in a profoundly religious home. Her mother had read to her many inspiring stories of the saints. She became enamored of them. After her mother's death, Teresa began to read romantic novels. It was her involvement in the fantasies of the romantic novels that prompted her father to want to make sure that she got a solid formation at the Augustinian school.

The second period of Teresa's spiritual life began with her schooling at the hands of the Augustinian nuns. Teresa voluntarily embraced an intensive asceticism. She aspired to heroic virtue. This prompted her at first to want to be an Augustinian and then eventually to enter the monastery of Carmel. The spirit of faith that surrounded her approach to her sickness at Carmel continued to deepen her commitment to the Lord and religious life. But then after the experience of her healing, she began to let prayer slip and became occupied in mundane dimensions of the convent life. As she admitted later in life, her curiosity sought out news and rumors about all that was happening in the life of her hometown and the wider world. During these years, she experienced dryness in her prayer and found it very difficult to persevere in it.

In 1554 Teresa seemed to move into a new phase in her life. God used the words of a spiritual director to invite her to a more radical conversion. She recognized the importance of freeing up the depths of her interior self for God. From this point on, there would be no tolerance for half-hearted efforts in her relationship with God. She wanted to belong entirely to him. At this point, God began to give special grace to her.

Dissatisfied with the imperfect way in which the life of Carmel was being lived in Ávila, she began to introduce recommendations for reform. These were not easily accepted in her own monastery. In 1560 Teresa established the first independent reformed Carmel and from 1562 to 1582 was responsible for a whole series of Carmelite foundations based upon this reform movement. Those who opposed her reform efforts reported her to the Inquisition. In 1578 she was investigated by the Inquisition. She voluntarily submitted everything that she had jotted down and encouraged those spiritual directors who had worked with her to talk freely with the members of the Inquisition. The judgment was totally in support of the soundness of her teaching. Four years later, God called her home.

Teresa's spiritual directors insisted that she put down in writing what she was becoming more and more aware of through her prayer. Thus, in 1561 she wrote the *First Book of Little Mementos*. In 1562 she made available her *Life*, taken from her journals. In 1569 *The Way of Perfection* appeared. In 1573 she completed her most systematic work, *The Interior Castle*. Finally, in 1581, *The Relations* recounted the work of the foundation of the reform Carmel monasteries.

Teresa wrote *The Way of Perfection* as a conversation with her Sisters in a series of conferences. It offers insights into life. It is not intended to be a presentation of a system of spiritual living. Originally, this work was not broken down into chapters. An editor later on undertook this task. *The Way of Perfection* reveals a good deal of Teresa's own inner life and supplements her autobiography.

The Teaching on Prayer

Underlying Teresa of Ávila's teaching on prayer is a constant encouragement to her disciples to be faithful to the discipline of prayer and to be as personally involved as possible in the prayer as well. She tried to move beyond the false dichotomy between developing habit and leaving prayer to spontaneity. She knew what had happened to herself in the course of her own life. Much of her teaching on prayer to her Sisters is rooted in her interpretation of the Lord's Prayer.

For Teresa, the underlying attitude of mind and heart necessary for an authentic relationship with God depended upon an appreciation that all we are and all we have come from God and are intended to be given back to him for others: "Now I think—unless one has a better opinion—that Jesus observed what he had given for us, how important it was that we in turn give this, and the great difficulty there is in our doing so, as was said, since we are the way we are; inclined to base things and with so little love and courage."[1]

This spirit of appreciation of our fundamental relationship with God should lead us to the spirit of adoration or worship: "Because everything I have advised you about in this book is directed toward the complete gift of ourselves to the Creator, the surrender of our wills to his, and detachment from creatures, I am not going to say any more about this matter" (32, par. 9).

Having established this foundational principle, Teresa then went on to indicate that increasing authenticity in prayer depends upon the awakening of the deeper desire in the human heart that God has already placed there for him. She was accustomed to speak of this desire in terms of a thirst:

> To me it seems that thirst signifies the desire for something of which we are in great want, so that if the thing is completely lacking, its absence will kill us. How strange that if water is lacking, this lack kills us; and if there is too much, we die, as is seen through the many who drown. O my Lord, who will find himself so immersed in this living water that he will die! (19, par. 8)

Later on in her treatise, Teresa described moving toward a prayer of quiet when competing desires that were warring in the human heart become less demanding and forceful. This comes about less through our own disciplined

[1] Teresa of Ávila, "The Way of Perfection", in *The Collected Works of St. Teresa of Avila*, vol. 2, trans. Kieran Kavanaugh, O.C.D. and Otilio Rodriguez, O.C.D. (Washington, D.C.: Institute of Carmelite Studies, 1980), 33, par. 2. Subsequent quotations are from this edition and will be cited in the text.

effort than our fidelity to the deeper desire for God and his grace making this possible.

Teresa made clear to her Sisters that silence was the condition for the deepening of the desire for God and the gradual diminishment of competing desires:

Now with regard to vocal prayer, you already know that His Majesty teaches that it is to be recited in solitude. This is what he always did when he prayed, and not out of any need of his own, but for our instruction. It has already been mentioned that one cannot speak simultaneously to God and to the world; this would amount to nothing more than reciting the prayer while listening to what is being said elsewhere or to letting the mind wander and making no effort to control it. (24, par. 4)

Teresa recognized that this is often a challenge for us in our human situation:

There can be exceptions at times either because of bad humors—especially if the person is melancholic—or because of faint feelings in the head so that all efforts become useless. Or it can happen that God will permit days of severe temptation in his servants for their greater good. (24, par. 4)

From her own experience, Teresa insisted on perseverance in prayer no matter how seemingly fruitless this prayer appeared to be at a given time in her life:

Well now, I say there are so many reasons why it is extremely important to begin with great determination that I would have to go on at much length if I mentioned them all. Sisters, I want to mention only two or three. One is that if we resolve to give something, that is, this little care, to someone who has given so much to us and continually gives—giving this little care is certainly to our advantage and we thereby gain so many wonderful things—there is no reason for failing to give with complete determination.... Another reason for beginning with determination is that the devil will not then have so free a hand to tempt. He is extremely afraid of resolute souls, for he has experienced the great harm they do to him.... The other reason for beginning with determination is—and it is very much to the point—that the person who does so struggles more courageously. He knows that come what may, he will not turn back. (23, par. 1 and 4)

Perseverance in prayer has to involve a willingness to include pain and suffering in our approach to life. For Teresa, God's allowing trials to enter our lives is his way of purifying and strengthening us:

When I think of this I am amused by persons who don't dare ask for trials from the Lord, for they suppose that in doing so, they will be given them at once.... For these are his gifts in this world. He gives according to the love he bears us: to those he loves more, he gives more of these gifts; to those he loves less, he gives less. And he gives according to the courage he sees in each and the love each has for his Majesty.... I myself hold that the measure for being able to bear a large or small cross is love. (32, par. 3)

Teresa was very realistic about the need to accept help when it was available:

There's one great blessing: you will always find someone who will help you, because this is a characteristic of the real servant of God to whom his majesty has given light concerning the true way; in the midst of these fears, the desire not to give up increases within him.... Oh, the greatness of God, for sometimes one or two men alone can do more when they speak the truth than many together! (21, par. 9)

Teresa through her own experience considered this a very important point. She was disappointed with confessors and spiritual directors who did not confront her with the truth. When asked if she had to choose between competence and holiness in a spiritual director, her response was unequivocally *competence*. She wanted someone who knew the truth and was able to speak it in offering guidance in the spiritual life.

In her commentary on the petition in the Lord's Prayer wherein we ask God to "forgive us our trespasses as we forgive those who trespass against us", Teresa spelled out her conviction that progress in prayer is dependent upon our willingness to forgive those who have hurt us. Holding on to resentments is a block to our own openness to God and his forgiveness of us (see 36).

Steps in Prayer

While Teresa in *The Interior Castle* presented in a more systematic fashion a survey of the journey of each of the stages she experienced in prayer, she presented in *The Way of Perfection* the initial stages of prayer in a more informal way.

For Teresa, the first step was coming to God with the real self:

> Leave aside any of that faintheartedness that some persons have and think is humility. You see, humility doesn't consist in refusing a favor the King offers you, but in accepting such a favor and understanding how bountifully it comes to you and being delighted with it…. Have nothing to do with this kind of humility, daughters, but speak with him as with a father, or a brother, or a Lord, or as with a spouse; sometimes in one way, at other times in another; he will teach you what you must do in order to please him. (28, par. 3)

In this same chapter, Teresa is utterly realistic about our need to pay attention to the body in prayer. The posture and the focus of the eyes are important. It is also important for us to realize that engagement in prayer, especially in the early stages, is going to be enervating for the body. Teresa claimed it was important to recognize the presence of God already in the soul: "I consider it impossible for us to pay so much attention to worldly things, if we take the care to remember we have a Guest such as this within us, for we then see how lovely these things are next to what we possess within ourselves" (28, par. 10).

After she addressed these fundamental dispositions of mind and heart for prayer, Teresa went on to suggest taking the very words that the Lord has given to us in his prayer as the subject of their personal prayer. Teresa encourages us to make sure that in offering a vocal prayer such as the Our Father there is genuine interior involvement in vocal prayer. To help draw out the meaning of this teaching, she then went on to offer a commentary of eleven conferences on the Lord's Prayer. These are contained in chapters 32 to 42 of *The Way of Perfection*. In this she imitated the approach taken by so many spiritual writers in the life of the Church before her.

Teresa wanted very much to help her disciples move from vocal prayer to what she called mental prayer. She claimed that mental prayer is very closely allied to vocal prayer entered into from the heart:

> Realize, daughters, that the nature of mental prayer isn't determined by whether or not the mouth is closed. If while speaking, I thoroughly understand and know that I am speaking with God and I have greater awareness of this than I do of the words I'm saying, mental and vocal prayer are joined. (22, par. 1)

As if to reinforce this teaching, she said in a humorous vein: "If, however, others tell you that you are speaking with God while you are reciting the Our Father and at the same time in fact thinking of the world, then I have nothing to say" (22, par. 1).

She encouraged her disciples to realize that the Lord is near and then to enter into his inner life to speak to him (see 28).

Teresa held that engagement in vocal and mental prayer should eventually lead to a prayer of quiet. In this prayer, the soul rests in relative peace and senses itself to be closer to God. The desire for union with God becomes stronger. The drives within us seem less compulsive. The interior faculties move a little bit more spontaneously toward God. The understanding seeks to know the Lord. The memory seeks to remember him alone. The will senses itself to be more resolutely drawn to him. The fruit of this prayer is a deeper union of the active and contemplative involvement in life. At first, moments of this prayer of quiet will be very fleeting. However, fidelity to prayer under God's grace can make them more common (see 31).

This development in prayer opens us to what Teresa considered *contemplation*. Unlike many other spiritual writers, Teresa restricted the term "contemplation" to special mystical grace from God. This grace, she testified, is not freely given to everyone. The journey that Teresa herself traveled is more explicitly described in her *Life*. She also attempted to present this in a more systematic way in the fifth, sixth, and seventh mansions contained in *The Interior Castle*.

Implications for Us

Teresa rightly helps us to focus on our personal engagement in prayer. Prayer cannot be the mere repetition of words. Prayer will be merely intellectual if the deeper part of ourselves is not involved. Only when we come to him precisely as we are, laying before him those dimensions of our lives that introduce obstacles for being able to come into his presence, do we free ourselves for a direct involvement with him. The center of our being, the heart, needs to be activated as we approach personal prayer and our celebration of the Eucharist. In our daily lives, a purity of heart that allows the deeper desire within us to become more active will help to support this desire and search for God. When we come to prayer, we want to bring to God all the concerns that we have, both the people in our lives and the tasks that are ours to accomplish, so that we can then be more fully open to him.

Obviously, the integration of prayer with life is fundamental. It is wrongheaded for us to see a dichotomy between habit and spontaneity in prayer. We need to engage in faithful practice and then make sure that our engagement is more and more from the heart. It is the nurturing of the desire for God that makes it more personal and our own.

Teresa offers a salutary message to all those who begin to live a religious life dedicated to God with generosity of heart and then begin to slip into mediocrity because of small compromises being made in life. Small compromises can lead to big ones, and big ones to scandal. Once the heart is pledged, it needs to be ever more fully given over to him through generous self-discipline and the courageous willingness to endure hardship for the Lord.

The obstacles to prayer that we face—our busyness, our anxiety, our competing desires, our fears, our lack of faith—provide the greatest temptations to us. Unless we are willing to release these concerns directly into God's hands, we will never persevere in prayer. Prayer is fundamentally a relationship with God, an experience in communion. We need to bring to God all of these *obstacles* that are experienced so that he, in turn, can strengthen us. The more the relationship with him is deepened, the more the concerns that otherwise seem to be stumbling blocks can become stepping-stones to God.

We are being called to share in the Trinitarian life. We need to let God truly be our Father. We need to approach him by allowing Christ to help us put on his own mind and heart. We need to pray through the gift of the Holy Spirit given to us to assist us in our prayer. We need to move beyond inflexible approaches to an open, truly human relationship with the Lord.

In our approach to prayer, simple conversation involving the depths of our own soul is best. In approaching meditative prayer, we want to begin by placing ourselves in God's presence, then move on to listening to his word with mind and heart, and finally asking for the grace to be able to respond to him with our whole soul.

Repetitive prayer in the Christian tradition has often been used to help the external senses of the body to be engaged in a rhythmical way while encouraging interior involvement in the mysteries of Christ and our relationship with God. In the Christian East, the Jesus Prayer has served this purpose. In the West, the Rosary has done this as well. In point of fact, the repetition of any word, particularly a scriptural word or phrase, can help to accomplish the same purpose. It is a way of bringing together the external senses in support of an interior engagement. To the extent that it does this for us, it can be a very helpful approach to prayer.

Lord Jesus, help me to pray. I want to approach the Father with you through the gift of the Holy Spirit dwelling within

me. I come with all the concerns, hopes, fears, and struggles of my heart. I place them in your hands. Help me to be attentive and receptive to your word. Help me to respond to you as you invite. Accept the time I spend in your presence as an expression of my love for you and my desire to be with you. Amen.

CHAPTER 9

The Sacramental Mystery

Catherine of Siena's Burning Desire

The movement into solitude nudges us into facing the "really real". Only in solitude do we have the opportunity to see God, ourselves, others, the world, and the demonic as they really are. But some people who introduce solitude into their lives become eccentric. It is because they have not appreciated in a balanced way the dignity and destiny of the human person. We are not asked to do harm to ourselves but rather to embrace a way of life that genuinely makes our own God's desire for us in creating us and redeeming us.

The nobility in which we have been created and for which we have been redeemed has been marred by sin. So conversion of heart and life is indispensable. This conversion, however, is intended to move us toward love. The love to which we are called is a love of self-gift rather than a love that is self-serving. It is a love to be realized in the ordinary events of our human lives. To do this we need order and purpose in our lives. We also need to confront realistically the seductions of the devil.

Our engagement with this journey in life involves real communion with God. So it is necessary that we introduce into our lives basic conditions for authentic prayer. This prayer will mature only in the face of difficulty and darkness.

We cannot address personal prayer without appreciating its profound relationship to liturgical prayer. For this let us turn to Catherine of Siena.

Catherine of Siena and Her Times

Catherine was born into the Benincasa family in Siena in 1347—the twenty-fourth of twenty-five children! (Unfortunately, only twelve survived infancy.) Her father, a wool dyer, was politically active in a city-state family racked by family feuds, class conflict, and revolution. He introduced Catherine early on in life to an appreciation of the wider concerns of the society in which they lived.

Catherine's mother was a woman deeply committed to God, to her husband, and to her children. Obviously, the responsibilities of such a large family presented innumerable challenges. She remained self-giving through them all.

Catherine had a strikingly pleasant and outgoing personality. She was imaginative and idealistic. In her early years, she was attracted to religious devotion, even though later on she was to condemn an exaggerated reliance on devotion that stood in the way of penetrating the deeper mysteries of faith.

Catherine experienced an intense emotional struggle between the possibilities of engaging in a life very much a part of this world and a more austere life she sensed herself called to live. Her family wanted her to marry and prepared her for the choice of a husband. In prayer she understood God to be asking her to make the choice for the more sacrificial way of life. Hence, she declined marriage and then began to introduce into her life the conditions for solitude and prayer.

Obviously, it was her family that first cultivated the lively faith that animated her. She also attended a school at San Domenico that was a center of learning and preaching run by Dominicans. There was a group of women called the Mantellate who were affiliated with the Dominicans. They wore simple garb, stayed in their own homes, and served the needs of the sick and poor. In consultation with the Dominican friars, Catherine decided to join them.

At twenty-one years of age, Catherine had a religious experience that had a determining impact on the rest of her life. She later described it as an invitation to mystical espousal with the Lord. Not only did she sense a call to a profound personal union with the Lord, but she also sensed that the Lord was asking her to become very active in the service of others. She served as a nurse in homes and hospitals, particularly during the Black Plague, which had such a devastating effect on her city. She cared for the destitute. Even while doing this, she preserved extended times alone for reading and prayer. She also introduced a disciplined way of life with regard to food and sleep.

Catherine learned a great deal from prayer. She experienced insight and courage coming from her prayer. Early on, she sensed that God was encouraging her to become a mediator among the political factions in the city of Siena. She also went to Pisa to persuade the people of both Pisa and Lucia to resist becoming a part of an antipapal league that was developing because of antagonism toward Pope Gregory's residence in Avignon. She tried to persuade soldiers who fought one another on the local scene to channel their military efforts into a crusade to try to bring the saving message of Jesus Christ back to the land that had been taken over by the Muslims. She wrote letters to English mercenary soldiers who were ravaging the Italian country-side and extorting money from the populace in an effort to try to persuade them to desist.

Her involvement in the political and military struggles of her times had very uneven results. This led her to move more deeply into the reform of the Church. She played a significant role in influencing Pope Gregory XI to move from Avignon to Rome. She established a monastery of strict observance of the Dominicans in Siena. She entered into some paraliturgical preaching at the invitation of Gregory XI's successor, Pope Urban VI. She went to Rome as a consultor to him and the Holy See.

Catherine wrote extensively to people in every walk of life. But her most important writing was her *Dialogue*. This emerged as the fruit of her prayer. In fact, *The Dialogue* is a report of the exchange with God that she experienced in her prayer. It is a powerful expression of the way in which one woman was transformed by her encounter with God through prayer.

The Dialogue

Catherine began *The Dialogue* by approaching God with four petitions. In the course of her prayer, she then sensed how God wanted to answer them. Her first petition was for herself that she might discover the truth and live her life in accordance with it. The second was for the reform of the Church. The third was for the whole world, especially the troubled spots about which she was aware in her own time. Fourth, she petitioned for the gift of divine providence regarding all human events, but in a special way for a particular situation that she did not mention publicly.

In the section of *The Dialogue* in which she begged God for the reform of the Church, Catherine sensed that God's response called her to come to a deeper appreciation of the Eucharist and the other sacraments of the Church. She learned in her prayer that it was important to be able to go beyond a love of God that was basically self-serving. Catherine heard God revealing to her:

> There are others who become faithful servants. They serve me with love rather than that slavish fear which serves for fear of punishment. But their love is imperfect, for they serve me for their own profit or for the delight and pleasure they find in me. Do you know how they show that their love is imperfect? By the way they act when they are deprived of the comfort they find in me and they love their neighbors with the same imperfect love. That is why their love is not strong enough to last.[1]

Catherine also recognized how fear of suffering can paralyze us in moving forward in the spiritual life. Again she heard God speaking:

> The first souls I spoke of failed because of their fear of suffering. These second grow lax, desisting from the service they were giving their neighbors and pulling back from their charity if it seems they have lost their own profit or some comfort they had formerly found in them. (60)

Catherine was drawn to truth. For her the truth was not abstract. It was the Lord himself. She understood that insight into the truth was a gift. She described it as food:

---

[1] Catherine of Siena, *The Dialogue*, trans. Suzanne Noffke (New York: Paulist Press, 1980), 60. Subsequent quotations are from this edition and will be cited in the text.

This food gives more or less strength according to the desire of those who receive it, whether they receive it sacramentally or virtually. *Sacramentally* is when one communicates in the holy sacrament. *Virtually* is communicating through a holy desire, both in longing for communion and in esteem for the blood of Christ crucified. In other words, one is communicating sacramentally in the loving charity one finds and tastes in the blood because one sees that it was shed through love. And so the soul is inebriated and set on fire and sated with holy longing, finding herself filled completely with love of me and of her neighbors. (66)

Catherine described what she experienced one morning when she went to church for Mass. This is how she understood God to reveal himself to her:

I revealed this to you when you had set yourself to resist the battle the devil was giving you in this sacrament, to make you grow in love and the light of most holy faith. You know that you had gone to the church at dawn to hear Mass, and before that the devil had been tormenting you. You went to stand at the altar of the crucifix, though the priest had come out to Mary's altar. You stood there considering your sinfulness, fearing that you might have offended me while the devil had been troubling you and you were considering also how great was my charity that I should have made you worthy to hear Mass at all, since you considered yourself unworthy even to enter my temple. When the celebrant reached the consecration you looked up toward him and at the words of consecration I revealed myself to you, you saw a ray of light coming from my breast, like the ray that comes forth from the sun's circle yet never leaves it. Within this light came a dove, and the dove and light were as one and hovered over the host by the power of the words of consecration the celebrant was saying. Your bodily eyes could not endure the light and only your spiritual vision remained, but there you saw and tasted the depths of the Trinity, wholly God, wholly human, hidden and veiled under that whiteness. (111)

Catherine experienced herself drawn deeply to the Eucharist. She initially experienced this as difficult, but it became easier as she recognized the relationship between personal prayer and liturgical prayer. This, too, was revealed to her in prayer:

How is this sacrament tasted? With holy desire. The body tastes only the flavor of bread, but the soul tastes me, God and human. So you see, the body's senses can be deceived, but not the soul's. In fact, they confirm and clarify the matter for her [that is, the soul], for what her mind's eye has seen and known through the pupil of holy faith, she touches with the hand of love. What she has seen she touches in love and faith. And she tastes it with her spiritual sense of holy desire, that is, she tastes the burning, unspeakable charity with which I have made her worthy to receive the tremendous mystery of this sacrament and its grace. (111)

When Catherine brought to God her concern for priests who did not live their lives and ministry well, God revealed to her that the most important way in which she was going to contribute to redemption was to touch the inner mystery of faith and to help priests to do the same. She was to focus on the mysterious way in which God pours out his love through the sacraments by her faith, and by this approach to the sacraments she would assist priests to come to appreciate the significance of what they are called to minister (see 120).

Catherine learned in prayer to appreciate in a particular way the significance of Christ's blood poured out for the redemption and transformation of the world. She sensed that God was asking her to become interiorly united with a self-sacrificing redemptive love unto death as the most important way to participate in the life of the Church. She recognized in prayer that after creation, salvation was the greatest gift God has given. Sin is the greatest evil. Conversion is the greatest need for all. The blood of Christ poured out on Calvary and sacramentally made present and available for Christians of every generation offers that gift of redemption.

Implications for Us

The Second Vatican Council has initiated in the Church a dramatic reform of the rites of our Sacred Liturgy. The immediate postconciliar years have been marked by efforts to implement the Council's Constitution on the Sacred Liturgy. Refinements of this reform have continued to our present day.

No external changes in the Liturgy, however, can of themselves effect the renewal of God's people. It is the message that Catherine of Siena learned in prayer that is most important. Our engagement with the Liturgy is primarily interior. The *desire* that we bring to become interiorly involved in the sacred mystery that is celebrated ultimately makes the difference. We are going to be bored unless we come with a burning desire to hear God's word, to meet him in sacrament, and to be changed in the way in which we continue to live our lives.

How important it is for us to bring to the Sacred Liturgy all that is transpiring within our own lives. We can then bring it directly to God and place it in his hands and offer ourselves in a way that is open and pliable to his loving will. We want to be taught by him. We want to be purified by him. We want to be changed by him. For this to happen as Catherine teaches us, we have to move beyond wanting to be entertained or made to feel good. Rather, we need to be strengthened by a voluntary self-offering in union with Christ that accepts the kind of suffering that purifies and ennobles us.

This kind of engagement in the Liturgy is what Liturgy ultimately implies. Liturgy is ultimately an involvement that demands courage and a lively faith. It requires the desire of the whole person to be engaged. It includes a willingness to be transformed and led into a new life.

This message is a particularly powerful one for priests. The very closeness to sacramental life and all that is holy that the priest experiences can, unfortunately, lead to a perfunctory attitude and approach. The renewal of priestly faith and life depends upon an ever-deepening engagement with the mysteries that he celebrates. If the priest is going to help others appreciate and enter into sacramental mystery, he first of all needs to contemplate this mystery in faith and celebrate the sacraments with reverence.

Lord Jesus, you make yourself available in sacrament in a wonderfully mysterious way. You want me to come to you with a burning desire to listen and heed your word. You want me to come to you with the kind of earnestness that enables me to be touched by your sacrificial love and impelled by that love to reach out to others in your name. Help me to enter into each Mass with the expectation that this will be a moment of sacred encounter and challenge

for life. Help me to come to you wanting to be molded by you, wanting to be forgiven, healed, transformed, and then challenged. May the Holy Spirit that transforms the gifts of bread and wine into your Body and Blood also transform me that I may be more fully incorporated in your saving life in the Church for the world. Amen.

CHAPTER 10

A Life of Virtue

The Devout Life of Francis de Sales

Solitude in the Christian spiritual life is but a means to a deeper and richer goal. That is why we need to remind ourselves of the way in which God has created and called us and destined us to live with him. Despite the original fall, we have within us his continuing image. Conversion in life helps to restore the likeness.

The development of the life of charity has to be at the heart of the Christian life. It is very challenging to develop. Love can be sidetracked in so many different ways. For us truly to mature, we need to develop a disciplined way of life with adequate supports to nurture the right way of loving. We also need to be utterly realistic about the presence and power of the demonic, for we can be misled so easily.

The life of prayer is intended to foster genuine communion with the Lord. This communion should strengthen and deepen our sense of God's love for us and our desire to love him above all. It is best experienced and expressed in the Eucharist. But the love of God is genuine only if it is also expressed in a love of others.

When we treated the teaching of St. Teresa of Ávila in *The Way of Perfection*, we recognized that the ultimate test of prayer is the degree of virtue that becomes manifest in our lives. Teresa used the image of water to express the grace of prayer. For her, prayer was ultimately sterile if it did not bear fruit. Water is intended to provide nourishment so that the soil can produce healthy plants. For Teresa, healthy plants were the virtues. To help us appreciate better the way to grow in the life of virtue, we will turn to St. Francis de Sales and his *Introduction to the Devout Life*.

The Life and Times of Francis de Sales

Francis de Sales lived in the second half of the sixteenth century and the beginning of the seventeenth. The second-generation Protestant reformers were his contemporaries.

Within the Church, the Catholic Counter-Reformation had already taken hold. The Council of Trent began in 1545, and over a period of eighteen years, there were three different extended sessions. It concluded its work in 1563. There had been a twenty-five-year delay before the start of the Council because of a structural dispute over the presence of the pope and the role of the laity. There also had been a conflict over the authority that Sacred Scripture would be expected to have in resolving the issues that the Council participants would be addressing. In the first session, the Council members addressed the role of Sacred Scripture and tradition, preaching, and the doctrine of justification. In the latter two sessions, the participants took up the issue of the sacraments and then the reform decrees that were to address pastoral discipline in the Church.

Following the Council, considerable confusion continued within society and the Church. Heroic and saintly reformers ultimately championed lasting renewal within the Church: Philip Neri, Jane Frances de Chantal, Louise de Marillac, Francis de Sales, Vincent de Paul, Charles Borromeo, Ignatius of Loyola, John of the Cross, and Teresa of Ávila.

Francis de Sales was born in the town of Thorens in Savoy in 1567. As a young man, he studied humanities and philosophy at the Jesuit College of Clermont in Paris. While he was a student there, he suffered depression and a serious temptation to despair. The ministry of a priest helped him move through this experience and ultimately planted the seed of a vocation to the priesthood.

However, after completing his undergraduate studies, Francis acquiesced to the hopes and expectations of his father and studied law at the University of Padua. In order to respond to some of the inner attraction he was experiencing, he also studied theology at the same time. He completed his studies at the University of Padua with a degree in both civil and canon law. Soon thereafter he was admitted as an advocate before the senate of Chambry. Then he presented himself to the bishop at Annecy and was ordained a priest.

Francis began his priestly ministry at Chablais. He tried to strengthen the life of the Catholic community. He also reached out in a warm and engaging way to the Calvinists. During this time, he wrote his *Controversies* and also his *Defense of the Standard of the Holy Cross*.

In 1599 Francis became the coadjutor bishop of Geneva. In 1604 Francis met Jane Frances de Chantal after preaching Lenten sermons at Dijon. She then sought him out as a spiritual director. Eventually, he assisted her in the foundation of the Visitation nuns.

Francis' first spiritual work was the treatise *On the Love of God*. He then wrote a rule of life for the Institute of the Visitation Sisters. Finally, in 1609, he published the *Introduction to the Devout Life*. Francis died in Lyons in 1622.

The Teaching of the *Introduction to the Devout Life*

Francis de Sales was an eloquent speaker. He was convinced that good preaching was the most important way to help the ordinary layperson come to know, love, and respond to the faith. He moved throughout the diocese preaching in the various parishes and in many instances offering weekend parish retreats. Following these, some people would write to him for spiritual direction in living a deeper life. Francis tried to respond to these requests. The *Introduction to the Devout Life* grew out of letters written to instruct people in the way of perfection. One of these recipients, Madame de Charmoisy, urged him to publish his letters. Francis redid the letters in chapter form to convert them into a book.

The underlying teaching in Francis de Sales' writing was that the way of holiness was open to all no matter what their role in life. All people need to do is to develop a genuine hatred for sin, a detachment from things of this world, a love of God, and a constancy in prayer. He urged those to whom he wrote to nurture an ever more generous love of God and an absolute confidence in him.

There are five books in the *Introduction to the Devout Life*. Book I treats the fundamental realities in the Christian life. Book II offers an introduction to prayer, spiritual exercises, the Eucharist, and confession. Book III focuses on the practice of virtue. Book IV treats counsels against the usual temptations, while Book V presents meditations and instructions to strengthen people in the life of virtue.

The Teaching on Virtue

Francis de Sales identified three fundamental principles in the development of the life of virtue. First, he tells us: "In the exercise of the virtues we should always prefer that which is most conformable to our duty, not that which is most agreeable to our tastes." Second, he stated: "Among the virtues connected with our particular duty, we must prefer the more excellent to the more showy." Third, toward the end of the same chapter, he taught:

> When assaulted by any vice we must embrace the practice of the contrary virtue as much as we can, and refer all others to it. By this means we shall overcome our enemy and at the same time advance in all the virtues. Thus, if assaulted by pride or by anger, I must in all my actions yield and turn toward humility and meekness and adapt all my other exercises of prayer and the sacraments, of prudence, constancy, and sobriety to this end.[1]

These simple yet profound maxims contain foundational wisdom for the life of virtue.

For Francis, humility is the most fundamental of the moral virtues. In an amusing passage, Francis cuts to the quick:

> We call glory that which we assume to ourselves, either for what is not in us, or for what is in us but not of us, or for that which is in us and of us but does not deserve that we should glory in it. The nobility of our ancestors, the favor of great men, and popular honor are things that are not in us. They are either in our ancestors or in the esteem of other men. Some men become proud and insolent because they ride a fine horse, wear a feather in their hat, or are dressed in a fine suit of clothes. Who does not see the folly of this? For if there be any glory in such things, the glory belongs to the horse, the bird, and the tailor! (III, 4)

---

[1] Francis de Sales, *Introduction to the Devout Life* III, 1, trans. and ed. John K. Ryan (New York: Doubleday Image, 1955). Subsequent quotations are from this edition and will be cited in the text.

For Francis the best way to discern sincerity is this: "So also if you would know whether or not a man is truly wise, learned, generous, and noble, observe whether his qualifications tend to humility, modesty and submission. For then they shall be good indeed" (III, 4).

Finally, Francis made clear that humility rests on truth, not affectation:

> I would pretend to be neither a fool or a wise man. For if humility forbids me to play the sage, candor and sincerity also forbid me to counterfeit the fool, and as vanity is opposite to humility, so artifice, affectation and dissimilation are contrary to honesty and sincerity. (III, 5)

Francis considered meekness in life important for the control of the aggressive drive:

> We must indeed constantly and courageously, but with meekness and compassion, resist evil and restrain the vices of those that are under our charge. Nothing so soon appeases the enraged elephant as the sight of a little lamb, and nothing so easily breaks the force of a cannon shot as wool. (III, 8)

Francis recognized that the correction of others in anger leads to fear, not love. He also recognized the folly of turning anger in on ourselves: "In this many are greatly to blame, who, on being overcome by anger, are angry for having been angry, troubled at being troubled, and vexed at being vexed. By this means they keep their heart drenched and steeped in passion" (III, 9).

Francis echoed the teaching of John of the Cross in his treatment of desires. He recognized that the failure to discipline our desires leads to agitation and frustration in our lives. The desire for honor, for money, and for acclaim eats away at our capacity to focus on what is true and good and noble. When we seek such, we become agitated within. When we fail to gain them, we become depressed. The pursuit, however, of the true, the good, and the beautiful brings peace (see III, 37).

It is important to note that Francis considered the proper way to discipline desire to be interior rather than exterior:

> As for myself, Philothea, I could never approve of the method of those who, to reform a man, begin with his exterior, such as his gestures, his dress, or his hair. On the contrary, it seems to me that we ought to begin with his interior. "Be converted to me," said God, "with your whole heart." (Prologue, 23, 26; III, 23)

In this treatise, Francis also recognized that the Gospel's call to simplicity of life is open to all. It is not necessary for us to dispossess ourselves of everything in order to be poor in spirit as St. Francis taught pointedly: There is a difference between having poison and being poisoned.

But Francis was also realistic about the need to be generous with what we have:

> Be more careful than worldly men are to make your good profitable and fruitful. Tell me, are not the gardeners of great princes more careful and diligent in cultivating and beautifying the gardens submitted to their charge than if they were their own? And why? Because without doubt they considered them as the gardens of princes and kings, to whom they desire to make themselves acceptable by their services. My Philothea, our possessions are not our own. God has given them to us to cultivate, and He wishes that we should render them fruitful and profitable. (III, 15)

In the *Introduction to the Devout Life*, Francis echoed the teaching of Aelred of Rievaulx regarding the difficulties of false friendships. In false friendships, people are drawn together for either superficial or immoral purposes. He pointed out what is at the heart of true friendship: God takes first place and the genuine good of the other is nurtured in each person. He proposed ways to differentiate between good and bad friendship and suggested guidelines for the handling of friendship in a life-giving way. In this context, Francis treated the call to holiness in married life. He also urged modesty and chaste living for all.

Implications for Us

It is dangerous to experiment either with God or with the devil. When we take prayer seriously, this should lead to a changed way of living. In cultivating openness to God and resistance to the devil, the fruit should be found in the life of virtue. Prayer is really an integral part of our life only if it is leading to a change in the way in which we live.

There is nothing more unattractive to those who are not believers than finding people who engage in worship and prayer not living a life of virtue. Religion can sometimes be used as a cloak for hostile and judgmental behavior. It is possible for people to say prayers without entering into true communion with God. Prayer leading to communion has to lead to a change in the way in which we live. True engagement with God has to lead to virtue in life. Failure to develop appropriate virtue can be a source of great scandal to others and may deter them from embracing the struggle themselves.

Division in our heart needs to be continually addressed. Conversion of heart is the process of gradually enlisting all of the forces of our being in the love and service of God and one another. It is the heart that opens us to depth.

Developing an authentic life of virtue has a great deal to do with looking at the simple, ordinary activities of our lives. There are small ways in which we can make choices about the way in which we live. Wisdom helps us to recognize the factors about which we can make choices even as we distinguish them from the factors over which we have no choice. Humility helps us to grapple realistically with ourselves, others, and the realities around us.

One of the dangers in our own age is superficiality. We can underestimate the importance of moments of solitude and prayer. Those moments open up greater depth. But there is also a danger if we engage in prayer and do not relate it to the rest of our lives.

In choosing the virtues that we most want to cultivate, it is important to look at our responsibilities in life. The sacrifices and the consequent virtues involved in fulfilling them are primary. A humble willingness to accept correction and suggestions from others will help us along the way. Most of all, the cultivation in prayer of a heart truly open to God's grace and sincerely desirous to act on his word will help to strengthen the life of virtue.

Lord Jesus, I want to belong to you and to live the new life you offer to me. Draw me closer to you that I may learn your way of thinking, judging, and acting. Touch me by your love that I may love others humbly, patiently, and perseveringly. Help me to do the ordinary in life extraordinarily well. Cultivate the life of virtue in me that I may express better to others the wondrous way in which you love them. Amen.

CHAPTER 11

Discerning Our Place in the World

Ignatius of Loyola's *Spiritual Exercises*

Our movement into a regular experience of solitude has helped us to be more truthful and real about the central realities in life. As we laid the foundation for our response to these realities in a correct Christian anthropology, we recognized that we have been created in God's image and likeness. This image is not merely found in the heart, mind, and will. It is also reflected in the way in which, as human beings, we share one human nature while existing as distinct human persons. This is reflective of the divine reality: God is one divine nature in three distinct divine Persons.

The original fall has led not only to personal disorientation but also to a disorientation in the way in which we live with one another. Conversion must therefore touch our life with one another as well. That is why the Christian writers have insisted that the spiritual journey is not an individualistic pilgrimage. It is shared with fellow Christian disciples. The life of charity is not tested except as it is lived out with others.

The disciplined way of life we need to cultivate then is rooted in a self-abnegation that moves us toward self-gift.

Our resistance to the seductions of the demonic has to be focused not only on our personal lives but also on the way in which the devil commonly operates in the world.

Sustaining and deepening our life of prayer leads us to the communal expression of it in sacramental life. The Eucharist is the source and the summit of this communal worship.

The life of prayer and worship has to be expressed in virtue if it is to be authentic. This virtue also is not merely personal. It has to be profoundly related to those around us and especially those in need. To help us appreciate better how to take responsibility for our own personal vocation in the world, we will turn to St. Ignatius of Loyola and the *Spiritual Exercises*.

Ignatius of Loyola and His Times

Ignatius was a contemporary of Martin Luther. Accustomed as we are to the mass communications of our day, we may find it difficult to appreciate how the tumultuous developments in Germany, France, and Switzerland left Spain untouched. Instead, the Iberian Peninsula was marked by a number of other spiritual movements. Some of these promoted questionable religious experience. Hence, this atmosphere set the stage for the emergence of a man who would make a significant contribution toward the authentic clarification of whether religious experience comes from God or the Evil One.

Ignatius was born in 1491 of an aristocratic family in the Basque section of modern-day Spain. In 1507, at sixteen years of age, he went to live with a relative who was attached to the royal court of Philip the Fair. Here he entered fully into the worldly life of this court. It involved gambling, dueling, and romancing. He fell in love with a woman of royal rank. Some speculate that it was a daughter of Philip the Fair.

In 1517 Ignatius entered the Basque army. He suffered a serious leg wound at Pamplona (or Pampeluna, as it was called then). This led to surgery and to an extended convalescence. While recovering in the home of a friend, he became bored and sought out some reading. The only books available in the house were one on the life of Christ and another on the lives of the saints. Luis Gonzales provides an account of what happened in his *Life of St. Ignatius*:

> By constantly reading these books he began to be attracted to what he found narrated there. Sometimes in the midst of his reading he would reflect on what he had read. Yet at other times he would dwell on many of the things which he had been accustomed to dwell on previously. But at this point our Lord came to his assistance, insuring that these thoughts were followed by others which arose from his current reading.
>
> While reading the life of Christ our Lord or the lives of the saints, he would reflect and reason with himself: "What if I should do what St. Francis or St. Dominic did?" In this way he let his mind dwell on many thoughts; they lasted a while until other things took their place. Then those vain and worldly images would come into his mind and remain a long time. This sequence of thoughts persisted with him for a long time.
>
> But there was a difference. When Ignatius reflected on worldly thoughts, he felt intense pleasure; but when he gave them up out of weariness, he felt dry and depressed. Yet when he thought of living the rigorous sort of life he knew the saints had lived, he not only experienced pleasure when he actually thought about it, but even after he dismissed these thoughts, he still experienced great joy. Yet he did not pay attention to this, nor did he appreciate

it until one day, in a moment of insight, he began to mar-
vel at the difference. Then he understood his experience:
thoughts of one kind left him sad, the others full of joy.
And this was the first time he applied a process of reasoning to his religious experience. Later on, when he began
to formulate his spiritual exercises, he used this experience
as an illustration to explain the doctrine he taught his disciples on the discernment of spirits.[1]

Ignatius was to identify this experience as the moment
when God nudged him from a childish approach to the
Christian life toward an adult embrace of that life. After
reading about the life of Christ and the saints, he became
intrigued with the significance of selecting or *electing* the
walk of life that God was calling him to fulfill. He was
very aware of an interior conflict between the desire
for noble and generous dedication on the one hand and
the attractions of the world and the flesh on the other.
He resolved to make a pilgrimage to Jerusalem. His first
stop was at Montserrat, where there was a Benedictine
monastic shrine to Our Lady. He gave away his possessions. He clothed himself in pilgrim's sackcloth. He made
a general confession.

Ignatius had intended to move from Montserrat to
Barcelona to board a ship for the Holy Land. He was,
however, unable to go because of a plague in Barcelona.
He therefore remained ten months in the nearby town
of Manresa. This forced an unwelcome delay. However,
he began to use the unexpected time for extended periods of prayer. He wrote down what he was experiencing.
This led him to some decisive meditations that ultimately
impacted the development of the *Spiritual Exercises*.

---

[1] Luis Gonzalez, *Life of St. Ignatius*, Chap. 1, 5–9, in *Acta Sanctorum* (July 7,
1868), 647.

Ignatius eventually did proceed to Jerusalem. He then returned and presented himself for philosophical studies in Alcala and continued both philosophical and theological studies at the University of Paris. While in Paris, he was inspired to consider the possibility of bringing together companions who, like him, wanted to take seriously the following of Jesus Christ. He desired to form a small society of men who would seek ordination and then serve in an active apostolic outreach to people in the world. They would neither be committed to a diocese for parish ministry nor confined to monasteries. They would take seriously the need to bring the Christian life into the world. He therefore went to Rome and secured papal authorization for the formation of the Society of Jesus.

The *Spiritual Exercises*

Ignatius wrote the *Spiritual Exercises* as an instrument to help people recognize and respond to the vocation given to them by God in life. The plan for the *Spiritual Exercises* grew out of Ignatius' own experience at Manresa. But the specific development of its details and the specific guidance given to those who were to lead others in the spiritual exercises became refined in the course of further experience.

The *Spiritual Exercises* are designed for a four-week experience of solitude. The first week is devoted to the consideration and contemplation of sin. The second week focuses on the events of the life of Christ. The third treats the Passion and Death of the Lord. The fourth invites the retreatant into an appreciation of the Resurrection and the Ascension, as well as the mission given to the disciples. Ignatius begins his treatise with what he calls "*the first principle and foundation*":

Man is created to praise, reverence, and to serve God our Lord, and by this means to save his soul.

The other things on the face of the earth are created for man to help him in obtaining the end for which he is created.

Hence, man is to make use of them insofar as they help him in the attainment of his end, and he must rid himself of them insofar as they prove a hindrance to him.[2]

This exposition of the fundamental relationship between ourselves and God on the one hand and ourselves and all other created reality on the other provides the backdrop and spells out the fundamental dispositions of mind and heart to bring to the *Spiritual Exercises*. We are to acknowledge that God is truly God. There is no other. We are also to accept in faith that God has created every finite reality to help us in attaining the destiny for which we have been created. We are to use them insofar as they help us reach that destiny. We must forgo them to the extent that they are a hindrance. This holy detachment is intended to free us and enables us to be generous in our response to God.

Building on this foundation and principle, the retreatant is then led through a series of meditations and examinations of conscience into a conversion experience: meditations on sin in the world; the way in which sin tends to operate in people's lives; our own serious personal sin; death, judgment, and hell; and the lesser ways in which we tend to compromise with the way of the unredeemed world and thereby live mediocre lives. These meditations are intended to culminate in a general sacramental confession (see 45–90).

---

[2] Ignatius of Loyola, *Spiritual Exercises*, trans. Lewis Delmage (New York: Joseph Wagner, 1968), 23. Subsequent quotations are from this edition and will be cited in the text.

After having become enlightened as to the way in which sin tends to get a hold on our lives, not just personally but structurally in the environment in which we live, we are then invited to focus on the invitation to follow Jesus Christ more fully. Meditations on the invitation and then some of the principal mysteries connected with the life of Christ make up this second movement. Two meditations bring special focus to this movement. The first is a meditation on the kingdom of Christ and is intended to move us to the inner generosity and readiness to make whatever choice God is asking. The second meditation is that of the two standards. Its purpose is to clarify the fundamental decision that faces every one: to yield to Lucifer or to accept Jesus Christ. The presentation of this fundamental choice is at the heart of the *Spiritual Exercises*.

The third movement is an invitation to enter more fully into the Paschal Mystery. The focus is on a series of meditations that move us through the Passion and death of the Lord.

The final movement brings us to the Resurrection and Ascension of the Lord and the missioning of the disciples.

The meditation to pray for a greater love of God helps to predispose us to want to make the right choice out of generous love. Two previous meditations on the three classes of men and the three degrees of humility prepare us for this commitment of love. The three classes of men are marked by three groups who have received a considerable sum of money. One does nothing to face his attachment to money, waiting until death, which catches him off guard. The second actively seeks to become detached, while retaining the money. The third is willing to do whatever God wants.

In the meditation on the three degrees of humility, we are helped to recognize that it is possible for us to make three basic choices: first, to be willing to do anything that God wants in order to avoid serious sin; second, to be willing to avoid venial sin; or third, to do what God wants even if it involves dispossessing ourselves or surrendering even legitimate possessions in order to be simple and poor with the Lord.

The focus of these *Spiritual Exercises* is to dispose us interiorly to hear God's word and respond to him in a magnanimous way in this life. It is an invitation to relate prayer to service of God in the world. We are invited to take seriously the needs of the world and to take our place in response to God in society.

At the conclusion of his *Spiritual Exercises*, Ignatius offered to the retreat director a series of principles for guiding retreatants. Thus, for instance, he offered the rules for the discernment of spirits. Then he offered the rules for the distribution of alms. Finally, he offered rules for thinking with the Church. These principles make clear that Ignatius intended his *Spiritual Exercises* to foster not individualistic piety but a way of life that was truly social and ecclesial as well.

Some Implications for Us

The *Spiritual Exercises* of Ignatius of Loyola help us to appreciate the significance of being a responsible Christian in the world. The dignity of each human being is rooted in our creation, our redemption, and our destiny. The roots of what has gone wrong, not only in our personal lives but also in the life of the world, are clarified in the reflections on the nature of sin and its continuing virulence in society.

We are invited to recognize that rooted in the dignity of each human person is a special call. God invites us to take our place in the Church and in the world. As Christians we are invited by God not only to make a human contribution but also to do it in such a way that we manifest our conviction and our desire to help others appreciate that redemption and salvation are central in life.

Service to others in the world should be rooted in humility and charity. Humility helps us to recognize the uniqueness of our own personal call. Charity enables us to respond to that call with generosity and magnanimity. Justice in the Scriptures and in the teaching of Ignatius is profoundly connected with redemption. To the extent that we accept God's justification in Christ Jesus and enter into our life's calling in such a way as to become instruments of justification for others, we are engaged in promoting true justice in the world. Our willingness to dispossess ourselves, if that is what God wants in order to share with others who may be in need, enables us to follow Christ ever more closely. As we assume the responsibilities of our unique vocational call, we contribute to the whole Body of Christ. This has profound implications for social life. As we resist those disorientations that undermine personal and communal life, we are also instruments of God's justice in this world.

The fundamental principles of Catholic social teaching focus on the dignity and sacredness of each human person, the solidarity that we experience with one another, the communal character of the human vocation, the rightful ordering of human society, the promotion of the common good, active participation in the life of society, respect for the equality of other human persons, and the proper use and distribution of the goods of this world.[3]

[3] See *Catechism of the Catholic Church*, second edition (Vatican City: Libreria Editrice Vaticana, 1997), especially paragraphs 1928–42, 2419–49.

The Gospel also has important relevance for addressing issues of war and peace. War should always be a last resort after every other means has been pursued in order to try to right wrong. There needs to be a proportion between the evil that has been experienced and the evil that will take place in the engagement of war. There should also be a reasonable hope of success. In the prosecution of war, innocent civilians should never be targeted. We find ourselves in a new kind of conflict brought upon us by terrorist activities. It is important to bring careful discernment to the public decisions about engagement in hostilities and a very cautious appraisal of the impact for good to be derived from the expansion of any military response.[4]

Ignatius invites us in the *Spiritual Exercises* to face each of those responsibilities in a profoundly spiritual way. The resulting engagement with the issues of justice flows from within. Instead of attempting to achieve justice by the artificial engineering of society, we are called to a changed mind, heart, and way of life.

St. Ignatius was convinced that it was the change of the inner person that would most effectively help us to become engaged in the world in the way God wants us to be. A prayer that he encouraged retreatants to offer may appear at first glance to be individualistic in focus. In point of fact, however, it is deeply personal and transformative. It is intended to open the Christian to genuine engagement in the world:

> *Soul of Christ, sanctify me.*
> *Body of Christ, save me.*
> *Blood of Christ, inebriate me.*
> *Water from the side of Christ, wash me.*

---

[4] See ibid., 2309.

Passion of Christ, strengthen me.
O good Jesus, hear me.
Within thy wounds hide me.
Permit me not to be separated from thee.
From the wicked foe, defend me.
At the hour of my death, call me.
And bid me come to thee,
That with thy saints I may praise thee
   For ever and ever. Amen. [5]

---

[5] From the Roman Missal, pre-Vatican II prayer.

CHAPTER 12

Suffering

John of the Cross and *The Dark Night*

Fidelity to solitude never comes easily. It is, however, a fundamental, facilitating condition for taking the spiritual life seriously. As we have seen, it provides the opportunity for us to face more realistically who we are, who God is, who other people are, what the world is, and what the demonic is.

Approaches to the spiritual journey, however, have often been distorted by unsound teaching. Distortions are often rooted in an imperfect appreciation of the human person. The understanding of our humanity that undergirds the approach that we take makes all the difference in the world. That is why we continually seek to learn from God himself about the way in which he has created us in his image and likeness.

Unfortunately, this likeness was distorted by sin. This sin is not only inherited by each one of us, but it is also reinforced by the way in which we tend to live. So repentance, forgiveness, healing, and transformation become incredibly important. This needs to be expressed in the adoption of a self-giving love that truly reflects the teaching of the Lord Jesus and a way of life that translates that teaching into practice. It involves as well a realistic confrontation with the powers of the demonic at work in the depths of our own hearts.

With this groundwork laid, we then turned to a more explicit treatment of prayer. Prayer obviously can never be divorced from the rest of life. There are, however, special supports and approaches to prayer that can help us in deepening our communion with God.

Prayer is authentically Christian only if it leads to a life of virtue. Virtue involves both a personal and a social struggle.

Engagement in prayer and the life of virtue inevitably lead us to face some of the darkness within ourselves and within life. None of us can be faithful in placing ourselves before our God regularly and faithfully without coming face-to-face with the darker side of life. The Evil One uses this to try to discourage us. In point of fact, God wants to use this suffering to purify us. To help us understand this we will turn to John of the Cross.

John of the Cross

John was born in Fontiveros, Spain, about twenty-four miles northwest of Ávila. His father came from a wealthy silk-merchant family but was disowned for marrying a poor weaver. His father died young of a long and costly illness that impoverished the family.

When he was young, John's mother sent him to a catechism school run by the Augustinian Sisters. John eventually became an apprentice in carpentry, tailoring, sculpturing, and painting. He also worked as a health aide at a local hospital.

With the financial assistance of a local priest, John went from 1559 to 1563 to a Jesuit college, where he received a solid formation in the humanities. While there he sensed a vocation to religious life. Upon graduation he entered the Carmelites. He was ordained a priest in 1567.

John met Teresa of Ávila, then fifty-two years of age, at the time of his first Mass. She sensed in him a kindred spirit and soon persuaded him to become involved in the reform movement that she was spearheading.

John made his first foundation for the reformed Carmelite friars at Durelo in 1568. Soon thereafter he became involved in a conflict over jurisdiction for the reform and was temporarily imprisoned by his own brother friars. These were the darkest days of his life. Eventually, he was able to secure a separate province for the reformed Carmelites in 1580. After a life of considerable physical and emotional suffering, John died of an ulcerated back and legs at forty-nine years of age.

John was a man of both inner strength and sensitivity. He harbored a great concern for the poor because of his own experience with poverty as a child. He also preserved through life a great concern for the sick. Never a very healthy man, he manifested great compassion to those who suffered from ill health. In a special way, he reached out to those who were depressed.

John considered the love of God as the source of zeal for souls. He is quoted as saying: "Who has ever seen a person persuaded to love God by harshness?"

Faith, hope, and charity were at the heart of the spiritual direction that he gave to others. He was unafraid to work alongside of laborers. He preserved throughout life a love for nature.

John's most important writings were *The Ascent of Mount Carmel, The Dark Night, The Spiritual Canticle,* and *The Living Flame of Love.* He actually considered *The Ascent of Mount Carmel* and *The Dark Night* to be a single volume. After his death, a series of his *Letters, Counsels and Poems* were published as well.

The Teaching of John of the Cross

In the introduction to *The Ascent of Mount Carmel* and *The Dark Night*, John identified the purpose of his writing in these words:

> Our goal will be, with God's help, to explain all these points, so that everyone who reads this book will in some way discover the road that he is walking along, and the one he ought to follow, if he wants to reach the summit of this mount.... But I am inclined to believe that even if it were presented with greater accuracy and polish, only a few would find profit in it because we are not writing on pleasing and delightful themes addressed to the kind of spiritual people who like to approach God along sweet and satisfying paths. We are presenting a substantial and solid doctrine for all those who desire to reach this nakedness of spirit.[1]

In understanding *The Ascent of Mount Carmel* and *The Dark Night*, it is important to appreciate the fact that John of the Cross considered both treatises to be a commentary on a single poem of eight stanzas in length. He presented the poem at the beginning of both *The Ascent of Mount Carmel* and *The Dark Night*. He then moved on in the course of the first book of *The Ascent of Mount Carmel* to describe the difficulty that we experience when we begin to introduce ascetical practices in our lives. He called this the *active dark night of the senses*. In Books II and III of *The Ascent of Mount Carmel*, he treated what he called the *active dark night of the spirit*. It is here that the disciple has to face darkness in faith.

The Dark Night begins with an initial description of the continuing need for purification. John then went on

---

[1] John of the Cross, *The Ascent of Mount Carmel* and *The Dark Night*, in *The Collected Works of St. John of the Cross*, trans. Kieran Kavanaugh and Otilio Rodriguez (Washington, D.C.: Institute of Carmelite Studies, 1973), prologue, 59. Subsequent quotations are from this edition and will be cited in the text.

to speak of the *passive dark night of the senses* in Book I and Book II, chapters 1 to 3. In the remaining portion of Book II, he treated the *passive dark night of the spirit*. In each of these cases, he addressed the suffering that we experience first on a more physiological level, then on a more spiritual level that, despite our human preference, God asks of us in order to draw us into closer union with him.

John offered at the beginning of *The Ascent of Mount Carmel* an explanation of the multiple causes of the darkness or suffering we will experience. He indicated that at the beginning of the spiritual journey, as we begin to draw away from sin, we have to experience a withdrawal from the worldly realities that we have accustomed ourselves to enjoy. Then, along the way, we are going to be tempted to vacillate in our fidelity to the disciplined life. Finally, the goal of our journey is God, who is of such a different nature from ours that we must ultimately let go of our usual sensory and intellectual ways of knowing in order to meet him in deeper communion. Each of these experiences brings suffering, or darkness.

Inevitably, we are going to experience difficulty in accepting this suffering. Initially, we find ourselves very reluctant to accept it. We do not understand either ourselves or the true nature and purpose of suffering. Often we find ourselves without competent models and guides.

The Active Dark Night of the Senses

For John, the *active dark night of the senses* involved the deepening of our desire for God, accompanied by the voluntary taming of the appetites that tend to compete with this desire for God. He described this experience in these words:

As for the first, it is plain that the appetites are wearisome and tiring for man. They resemble little children, restless and hard to please, always whining to their mother for this thing or that, and never satisfied. Just as a man who digs covetously for treasure grows tired and exhausted, so does he who strives to acquire the demands of his appetites become wearied and fatigued. And even if he does finally obtain them he is still always weary because he is never satisfied. For after all, he digs leaking cisterns which cannot contain the water that slakes thirst. I, 6, 6

It is in this teaching that John makes clear that untamed appetites tend to blind us from the real truth. It is only in following a mortified way of life that we lay hold of deeper truth. That is why the Church has always taught that it is necessary to follow the Gospel way of life before we can deepen our understanding of the life-giving truth behind it. Those who fail to embrace this life then have a tendency either to reject or criticize the life-giving truths that the Church teaches. For the untamed appetites not only undermine the practice of virtue; they also blind the eyes of the soul.

In order to enter this effort, John made clear that there are two fundamental dispositions of mind and heart necessary: the desire to imitate Christ in all deeds by bringing our life into conformity with his; the willingness to renounce and empty ourselves of any sensory desire that is not of him and for the glory of God. To do this, John proposed a rather daunting challenge:

> Endeavor to be inclined always:
> Not to the easiest, but to the most difficult;
> Not to the most delightful, but to the harshest;
> Not to the most gratifying, but to the less pleasant;
> Not to what means rest for you, but to hard work;
> Not to the consoling, but to the unconsoling;
> Not to the most, but to the least. (I, 13, 6)

Notice that John was talking about the development of inclinations that are contrary to the disorientations that otherwise tend to enslave us. In order to avoid those enslavements, it is necessary for us to cultivate contrary desires. John was not saying to us that we should *always* choose the most difficult or the harshest or the least pleasant. He was simply saying that we should develop an inner openness and desire to be able to do that so that we can make the choices that God wants us to make. The ultimate purpose of this ascetical effort is for us to be inwardly free enough to be able to choose what God wants whether it is easy or hard, attractive or unattractive. He called this effort the *active dark night of the senses*. It is *active* because we voluntarily choose to attempt it. It is a *dark night* because we experience real deprivation. It is experienced in the *senses* because it involves physiological and emotional deprivation.

The Active Dark Night of the Spirit

John then moved on to the *active dark night of the spirit*. This is marked by the generous giving of ourselves to follow the law of Christ and of the Church, even when it is not fully understood. It involves the surrender of a clarity and certainty that is based on rational knowledge alone. It therefore involves going beyond what the human faculties can comprehend and appreciate. Our untamed spiritual appetite wants to be able to understand. John explained this phenomenon by drawing attention to the fact that a partially blind man can resist help because of his partial vision. So it is with us all.

In order to enter into this *active dark night of the spirit* the intellect has to surrender its need to understand fully the faith that we profess. We cannot insist on our own insight or judgment being superior to that of Sacred Scripture or the Church's teaching. We have to be willing to surrender the security that comes from inner spiritual consolations. Moreover, we must be willing to forgo accomplishing this by the use of our own will alone. God must enable this to take place.

In prayer this *active dark night of the spirit* is accompanied by a move beyond meditative prayer to a prayer of greater quiet. It may seem as though the prayer is less fruitful because the mind is less occupied. But if mind, will, and heart are focused actively on the Lord, wanting to belong to him and to do his loving will, this is truly a graced development in life.

John of the Cross called this experience *active* because with God's grace we need to choose it voluntarily. It is a *dark night* because we are deprived of the light of understanding. It is experienced in the *spirit* because the deprivation is on the level of the mind.

The Passive Dark Night of the Senses

In *The Dark Night,* John of the Cross then began to address the way in which some suffering we experience in life comes despite our own free will. He described the *passive dark night of the senses* as a deprivation on the physical and emotional level that is totally involuntary. We may experience dissatisfaction, not only with human realities but also with God. Physical and emotional comforts may be denied us against our will. We experience ourselves as wondering whether we really are serving God because we do not have an inner relish for the things of God. Our difficulty in prayer reinforces this fear.

St. John encouraged us in this situation to be willing to move beyond rational meditative prayer to a simple attentiveness to God. He invited us to be willing to endure the sense of fruitlessness. What is happening is that the roots of the capital sins are being seared away. It is like being weaned from our mother's breast. It represents a great step forward; yet there is a sense of significant deprivation. The experience is called *passive* because we do not choose it. It is a *dark night* because it involves suffering. It is suffering on the sensory level and hence described as a *night of the senses*.

The Passive Dark Night of the Spirit

Finally, John treated the *passive dark night of the spirit*. For him, this is the experience of darkness in the mind and dryness in the heart. It is experienced as emptiness. He assured us that there is a need to undergo this purification. If we do not experience it in this life, we will as a transitional stage in the life to come before entering into the fullness of glory. It is marked by fears and struggles, the sense of deprivation, and the feeling of being abandoned by God and fellow creatures. He used a powerful image to describe this:

> For the sake of further clarity in this matter, we ought to note that this purgative and loving knowledge or divine light we are speaking of has the same effect on a soul that fire has on a log of wood. The soul is purged and prepared for union with the divine light just as the wood is prepared for transformation into the fire. Fire, when applied to wood, first dehumidifies it, dispelling all moisture, making it give off any water it contains. Then it gradually turns the wood black, makes it dark and ugly, and even causes it to emit a bad odor. By drying out the wood, the fire brings to light and expels all those ugly and dark accidents

which are contrary to fire. Finally, by heating and enkindling it from without, the fire transforms the wood into itself and makes it as beautiful as it is itself. (10, 1)

St. John then reassures us that the fruit of patient perseverance in the face of this kind of suffering is the development of a new kind of intuitive understanding of God, a deeper and more faithful loving will, and an inner freedom to make an ever-greater gift for ourselves. Most people do not experience the depths of this in this life. However, John saw this as the normal process of purgation that in some form we all have to experience in order to be able to enjoy God forever. He called it *passive* because God is the agent. It is a *dark night* because of the suffering involved. It is *of the spirit* because it is experienced in the mind and will.

Implications for Us

In treating of suffering, we touch upon one of the most difficult mysteries in human life. All suffering is humanly abhorrent. We tend to resist it with every fiber of our being. The culture in which we live considers it something to be avoided at all costs. Lest the teaching of John of the Cross seem too sublime, let us draw out some practical implications for living the Christian life.

For instance, we tend as human beings to dislike self-discipline. We find it difficult to voluntarily give up something that we like. We may eat too much or drink too much. We may exercise too little. We may allow ourselves to become addicted to the television or human comforts. But we usually make a special effort in Lent each year to be faithful to some form of self-discipline. This is a real way of participating in the *active dark night of the senses*. We are actively and voluntarily depriving our senses of some satisfaction in order to strengthen our desire for a greater good. We know that our human cravings will begin to control us, unless we keep them in check.

Let us take another example. As human beings we are often inclined to balk at some of the more challenging Gospel messages or Church teachings. The more sophisticated we think we are, the more we may be inclined to become selective about the Church's teaching. Some may experience difficulty with the sacrament of penance or with Marian doctrine. Some may reject elements of the sexual or social moral teaching. John of the Cross would urge us to have the courage and the faith to enter the *active dark night of the spirit*. Faith is not the same as understanding. We need to be humble enough to accept truth that we do not yet understand if we are to progress toward spiritual maturity. We have to deny ourselves (our limited, imperfect selves) in order to gain life. It is only in living the truth in faith that we then begin to experience the inner understanding of it. But to do this takes a voluntary relinquishing of the human need to control life with the mind or to be master of our own lives.

Can we go further? We all experience the pain that comes from unwanted physical or emotional suffering. Sickness, stress, and disappointment can overwhelm us. We recoil from this and generally ask God to deliver us from it. Those without faith may even be tempted in the face of terminal illness to end their own lives rather than face any prolonged suffering. John of the Cross would consider this a challenge to enter the *passive dark night of the senses*. This is involuntary suffering. We cannot eliminate it. We are invited to unite ourselves with the heart of Jesus, who faced rejection, betrayal, false accusation, a rigged trial, torture, and a terribly painful death with redemptive love. He offered himself for the salvation of us all. He returned forgiveness for evil, saying: "Father, forgive them; for they know not what they do" (Lk 23:34). The greatest of evils—our killing of our God—became the greatest of goods: salvation offered to all who would accept it.

Finally, let us take the example of human tragedy. Inevitably, when such tragedy strikes, we ask the bigger question of why Why the holocaust or other contemporary expressions of genocide? Why the horrendous attacks against Americans on September 11, 2001? Why the personal loss of a child or a loved one? Tragic suffering tends to shake our faith in God. John of the Cross would encourage us not to fear the *passive dark night of the spirit.* We cannot understand what has happened. It makes no sense. Only our willingness to let God reveal his saving purpose, in time, can enable us to move through this kind of shattering experience in a saving way.

In this journey, we then discover that physical and emotional experiences are not fully reliable, although they do offer important clues to us as we live our human life. God intends a real transformation of our sense experience. Feeling and will are not the same thing. We must leave room for the purification of our feelings and the transformation of our wills so that we can truly respond to what God offers.

Intellectual knowledge must also leave room for the kind of graced intuitive knowledge that is far superior. There is an authentic knowledge that comes through faith and the embrace of the cross, but there will always remain some darkness in the mind. We will need to unlearn what we have previously learned in an imperfect way. We will need to recognize that all rational and even conceptual knowledge is ultimately inadequate to grasp God. We will need to recognize that radical attachment to God is not experienced through clarity of thought, image, or reasoning.

Although this teaching may in some way seem beyond us, it is important that we face the basic truth of it on an ongoing basis. When we experience suffering because we cannot have what we desire, we are experiencing a form of the *passive dark night of the senses*. When we cannot grasp or understand why events have happened in a way that seems tragic to us, we are experiencing a form of the *passive dark night of the spirit*. John of the Cross offered rich insights for entering into this mystery in a graced way.

Lord Jesus, everything within me resists suffering, however it may come to me. Humanly, I want to eliminate it as best I can. Help me to appreciate better how you experienced suffering and transformed it for all time. Help me to grow in a willingness to embrace the suffering you want for me so that I may be more closely united to you. Make possible within me what I cannot do on my own. Above all, transform the suffering by your purifying love so that I, in turn, may help others with their suffering, too. Amen.

CHAPTER 13

The Goal of Life

Jean-Pierre de Caussade and the Gift of Abandonment

When we take seriously the journey of the spiritual life as a follower of Jesus Christ, our goal is to seek not personal peace but rather an ever-greater capacity to make a gift of ourselves. Our movement into solitude was to introduce the condition for engaging with the full range of reality in life. Our understanding of God's creative and redemptive intentions for the human person revealed to us the richness, not only of human dignity but also of our destiny. The conversion to which we are called in life is a turning away from self-centered life and love to a self-giving life and love. Our attempt to introduce supportive conditions in our life and to grapple realistically with the enemy in life is intended to strengthen us for the long-term giving of ourselves in life.

Our serious engagement with prayer is intended to bring us into a life-giving relationship with the Lord. As we experience his personal and freeing love for us, we in turn are interiorly strengthened to want to love others as he has loved us. This needs to be expressed not only when life is going well but also in a particular way when we experience difficulty and challenge. Only then is virtue truly tested and developed. This virtue is not simply personal. It is communal and social as well.

So we now look to the goal of life. Since we ourselves are a gift of God, we are called to make a return gift of ourselves to him. This is to be done gradually in the course of our lives as we express that return gift of ourselves to him in our service to others. Ultimately, it will involve a total self-surrender to him at the end of our lives. To appreciate this more, we will turn to Jean-Pierre de Caussade.

De Caussade's Times

Teresa of Ávila, John of the Cross, Francis de Sales, and Ignatius of Loyola lived in the sixteenth century. Before that century was over, wars of religion ravaged Western Europe. In France, Catholics and Huguenots were at war. In the Netherlands, there was a split that led to the emergence of two separate countries, Holland and Belgium. The struggle between Anglicans and Roman Catholics in England became a bitter one. Then Methodists, Presbyterians, and Puritans eventually split off from the Anglican church. The attempt by Queen Elizabeth I to impose the royal supremacy and Anglicanism on Ireland led to the horrible penal laws and the consequent bitter antagonism of the Irish toward the English. The Thirty Years' War between Lutherans and Catholics marred German soil.

The Catholic Reformation, sometimes called the Counter-Reformation, emerged as an attempt to address renewal and reform within the Roman Church. The Council of Trent had already taken place. The implementation of the Council, however, took generations to realize. It was really the emergence of rather remarkable saints who spearheaded the reformation within the Church. Charles Borromeo, Philip Neri, Francis de Sales, Jane Frances de Chantal, Ignatius of Loyola, Teresa of Ávila, and John of the Cross were examples of this.

The seventeenth century was then marked by a significant Catholic revival. The Church began to focus her apostolate more on the education and formation of the lay members of the faithful and to serve those in need. Vincent de Paul and Louise de Marillac were examples of those instrumental in this revival. The Council of Trent had called for a reform of the life of the clergy and the preparation of candidates for ordination. Experiments in the development of the first seminaries took place under Charles Borromeo and Vincent de Paul. Religious communities underwent reform from within. Some communities died and others were born. Even the contemplative orders experienced renewal with the spread of the reform to the Carmelites and the founding of the Visitation Sisters.

Under the influence of a professor at the University of Louvain, Jansenius by name, an approach to spirituality developed that was to introduce some special difficulties in the Church. This approach became known as Jansenism. In reaction to the corruption within the Church, those who were committed to a very serious engagement with the spiritual life became attracted to the rigor of this Louvain reformer. Jansenius sought to return to Sacred Scripture, the Fathers of the Church, and especially the teaching of Augustine. He and his followers presented a very optimistic view of human nature before the fall, but a very pessimistic view of the same after the fall, especially with regard to free will. The disorientations within the human person consequent upon original sin seemed so powerful and so all-pervasive that the Jansenists saw no way of counteracting them or winning a victory over them except in a very disciplined form of asceticism and a rigid understanding of Catholic Christian spirituality. This form of asceticism attracted the idealistic, but it also led to a disregard for some of the basic human dimensions of Christian living.

Another movement within the Counter-Reformation came to be called Quietism. Its proponents took prayer very seriously. They wanted to help disciples move very quickly from the initial stages in prayer to a prayer of quiet. They fostered a basically passive stance before God and downplayed the role of active asceticism in life. Molinos was the chief proponent of this in Spain. In France it appeared in a more modified form under the inspiration and leadership of Madame Guyon, who was aided and supported by Bishop Fénelon. This approach, in neglecting sufficiently the need for conversion of heart and life, prompted people to claim to be led by the Holy Spirit without first having entered real conversion or the struggle to develop basic virtues.

The seventeenth century was also marked by a marvelous expansion of missionary activity. The Latin countries of Europe took an active role in exploring and then taking the Gospel to the newly discovered continents across the Atlantic Ocean. There was also extensive activity moving toward the East in Asia. This whole period was marked by a renewed sense of the importance of taking seriously the living of the Catholic Christian spiritual life.

The eighteenth century was strongly influenced by the emergence of the Enlightenment. In this movement, reason was exalted over faith. There was general disenchantment with the way in which religious conviction had led more to open conflict than to peace and cooperative efforts in life. Philosophers and political leaders became convinced that the restoration of reason to the governance of human affairs held out the greatest hope for dealing with the splintering of Christianity. Thus, there emerged a renewed enthusiasm for the exaltation of the human person and the intellect. Concomitant with this was a systematic attitude of suspicion toward religious tradition and traditional learning.

In response to this, the French school of spirituality provided the strongest source of renewal within the Church. This school, inspired by the work of Cardinal Bérulle, focused on the preparation and formation of the clergy. It also encouraged a deeper appreciation for the close relationship between sacramental life and the rest of human life.

In the second half of this century, the Society of Jesus came under strong attack and was ultimately suppressed from 1773 to 1814. It was perceived as having infiltrated government and royalty. It seemed to exercise significant power and prestige through the influence it had gained. It was, however, identified as anti-Jansenist among people who were basically favorable to a more disciplined if not rigorous approach to life. In moral theology, Jesuits had come to be seen as encouraging and fostering a less rigorous approach to Christian living.

Jean-Pierre de Caussade

We know relatively little of the life of Jean-Pierre de Caussade. He entered the Society of Jesus in 1693 and was ordained a priest in 1704. He taught Greek, Latin, philosophy, and physics from 1708 to 1714. Then he obtained a doctorate in theology at Toulouse.

Rather than accepting a professorship, de Caussade became an itinerant missionary and teacher. He served as spiritual director of the Visitation nuns in Nancy. Then he assumed the same role in the seminary in Albi and finally in the seminary in Toulouse. He became rector of the Jesuit college in Perpignan. However, progressive blindness introduced serious limitations in his capacity for pastoral ministry. He died in 1751.

Jean-Pierre de Caussade did not write for publication. However, a book entitled *On Prayer* eventually was published from his spiritual instruction on the various states of prayer in accordance with the teaching of Bossuet. After his death, a series of conference notes given to spiritual directees was edited and published under the name *Abandonment to Divine Providence*. A Jesuit priest by the name of Ramiére edited them by putting them in a readable fashion. Finally, a book entitled *Letters* appeared as a collection of some of the letters that de Caussade wrote to spiritual directees.

In his teaching, Jean-Pierre de Caussade drew richly on the teaching of St. Francis de Sales about the invitation given to all of the faithful to take seriously the life of Christian virtue and the call to holiness. He also depended greatly on the more challenging teaching of John of the Cross and the movement toward deeper prayer. In reading Jean-Pierre de Caussade, it is important to note that he was basically writing to those who already were partially advanced in the living of the Christian spiritual life. He therefore presumed the initial stages of conversion and the beginning developments of virtue.

The Teaching of *Abandonment to Divine Providence*

Jean-Pierre de Caussade echoed a consistent teaching in the unbroken Christian spiritual tradition, pointing out that it really does not matter what gifts are given to each of us or what walk of life we are called to live. Everyone is called to a life of holiness:

> This is why I preach self-abandonment and not any particular way of life. I love whatever is the state in which your grace places souls and have no liking for one more than another. I teach all souls a general method by which they can attain that state you have designed for them. I ask of them nothing but an eagerness to abandon themselves completely to your guidance, for you will lead them very surely to what is best for them. It is faith I preach to them: abandonment, confidence and faith. They must long to be subject to and the tool of God's action, believing that at every moment and through all things this action is at work for them according to the measure of their good will.[1]

According to the teaching of de Caussade, God's grace does the deepest and most real purifying of sin. Initially, we need to live in God and engage in an ascetical effort. But eventually, we must move into an experience where God more actively lives in us and he seems to be in command. De Caussade tells us:

> Sometimes we live in God and sometimes God lives in us. These are very different states. When God lives in us, we should abandon ourselves completely to him, but when we live in him, we have to take care to employ every possible means to achieve a complete surrender to him. These means are clear enough: courses of reading, self-analysis, regular examination of our progress—everything is done by rule.... But when God lives in

---

[1] Jean-Pierre de Caussade, *Abandonment to Divine Providence* 3, 7, trans. John Beevens (New York: Doubleday Image, 1975). Subsequent quotations are from this edition and will be cited in the text.

us, we have nothing to help us beyond what he gives us moment by moment. (3, 1)

The goal of the Christian spiritual life is to allow Jesus Christ to become the chief formative influence of our hearts through faith, hope, and charity:

> This state of abandonment is a blending of faith, hope and love in one single act which unites us to God and all his activities. When these three virtues are united, they of course become one and so form a single act, a single raising of the heart to God and the simple abandonment to him. (3, 3)

De Caussade therefore envisioned a gradual simplification of the inner activity of the heart. To the extent that the deepest desire for God becomes operative, there is a greater chance that this simplification of a faith-filled mind, a hope-filled heart, and the capacity for self-giving in the will come together in a unified way.

It is important to emphasize that Jean-Pierre de Caussade presumed the active and disciplined gift of self. To read de Caussade otherwise could lead us to think that his teaching was promoting a passive approach such as that taught by Fénelon or Guyon, to whom he took explicit exception. Jean-Pierre de Caussade placed significant emphasis on the need to enter into an active engagement with the responsibilities in life, the fulfillment of the precepts of God and the Church, and submission to the inspirations of divine grace: "To be actively loyal means obeying the laws of God and the Church and fulfilling all the duties imposed on us by our way of life" (1, 3).

Obviously, for de Caussade, the Christian life cannot simply be a personal journey. It should not be such for us either, since it involves taking seriously our participation in the life of the Church.

Jean-Pierre de Caussade placed a significant emphasis on abnegation, love, and obedience. He placed a great importance on the example of Mary:

> This was the hidden motive of Mary's behavior. She was the simplest of humans and the one who made the most complete surrender of herself to God. Her laconic reply to the angel—"Let what you have said be done to me" (Lk 1:38)—embodies all the mystical theology of her ancestors. This, then, as now, meant the most direct and wholehearted surrender to God's will, however it revealed itself. (I, 1)

He went on to indicate that there is a very real parallel between Mary's wholehearted response to the Father and the invitation that Christ has given to all of his disciples to do likewise:

> This noble and exalted frame of mind was the basis of Mary's spiritual life and reveals itself perfectly in those very simple words: "Let what you have said be done to me." We should note that they are in perfect agreement with those our Lord wants to have always on our lips and in our hearts: "Your will be done." (I, 1)

For de Caussade, the real obstacles are within the soul. God can always use external obstacles for his good purpose:

> No matter what her (Mary's) jobs were—ordinary, commonplace, or seemingly more important ones—they revealed to her, sometimes quite clearly, sometimes obscurely, the activity of the almighty and were an opportunity for her to praise God. Filled with joy, she regarded everything she had to do or suffer at any moment of her

life as a gift from him who showers delight upon those who hunger and thirst only for him and not for the things of the world. (1, 1)

De Caussade understood this kind of response to include a willingness to experience considerable suffering:

No thought, no mental effort will teach us anything about pure love. We can learn of it only through the activity of God, and God teaches us, both through our reason and through difficulties and setbacks. What we learn by these teachings is that there is nothing good except God. To know this we must get rid of all we hold dear. (4, 2)

Jean-Pierre de Caussade retrieved from the Christian spiritual tradition a very fundamental truth and gave it a new name. He pointed to the reality that God reveals himself through all there is, every single person, and every event that happens. He called this *the sacrament of the present moment.*

Faith sees that Jesus Christ lives in everything and works through all history to the end of time, that every fraction of a second, every atom of matter, contains a fragment of his hidden life and his secret activity. The actions of created beings are veils which hide the profound mysteries of the workings of God.... Yet, because it is invisible, we are always taken by surprise and do not recognize his operation until it has passed by us. If we could lift the veil and if we watched with vigilant attention, God would endlessly reveal himself to us and we should see and rejoice in his active presence in all that befalls us. At every event we should exclaim: "It is the Lord!" (2, 1)

It takes faith to recognize the presence of the Lord in the simplest of events. This is particularly true when the events are difficult: "God reveals himself to the humble in the lowliest of disguises, but the proud, who never look below the surface, fail to find him even in his greatest manifestations" (1, 2).

De Caussade even found himself shocked by the number of people who fail to approach God's action in human life more reverently:

> There is so much unbelief in the world, for too many people speak of God unworthily and never stop finding fault with his activities in a manner they would not dare use toward the most incompetent workman. What we really want to do is restrict his work so that it conforms to the rules and boundaries that our limited reason considers suitable. (2, 6)

At the heart of appreciating the teaching on the sacrament of the present moment is recognizing that God reveals his face most securely in the ordinary duties and responsibilities that are ours in the living of daily life:

> There is very little unusual about the outward life of the Blessed Virgin, or at least the Gospels do not record it. They show her life as very simple and ordinary. What she did and endured might have been done and endured by anyone in her station of life. She visited her cousin Elizabeth just as her other relatives did. Like all her neighbors, she went to Bethlehem to be registered. Because she was poor, she sheltered in a stable. The persecution of Herod drove her from Nazareth, but she returned and lived there with Jesus and Joseph, who worked to earn their daily bread. But what was the bread that nourished the faith of Mary and Joseph? It was the sacrament of the moment. (1, 2)

De Caussade was insistent that it is the development of an interior faith and a desire to recognize God revealing himself to us in the ordinary that makes the difference:

But what did they (Mary and Joseph) experience beneath an existence apparently filled with nothing but humdrum happenings? On the surface it was similar to that of everyone around them, but faith, piercing the superficialities, disclosed that God was accomplishing very great things. (1, 2)

For de Caussade, the secret was the following:

The common sense of ordinary souls is simply this: being perfectly satisfied with what it knows is suitable for it, and never attempting to tread beyond the boundaries laid out for it. It is not inquisitive about the way God acts. It is quite happy to submit to his will and makes no attempt to find out its intentions. It wants to know only what every moment says to it, listens to what God utters in the depths of its heart, and does not ask what has been said to others. (2, 12)

De Caussade recognized that there is a very important way in which Holy Scripture and books based upon Scripture help us to uncover God's revelation. But he wanted us to use them in relation to the simple ordinary events in our life:

We are really well taught only by the words which God addresses especially to us.... It is what happens moment by moment which enlightens us and gives us that practical knowledge which Jesus Christ himself chose to acquire before beginning his public life. The gospel tells us how he "increased in wisdom" (Lk 2:52), although, as God, all wisdom was already his. This knowledge comes to us only through experiences absolutely necessary if we want to touch the hearts of those God sends to us. (2, 8)

This revelation of God, unlike what is said in a more universal way in Sacred Scripture, is deeply personalized:

So we must listen to God moment by moment to become learned in this practical theology of virtue. Take no notice of what is said to other people. Listen only to what is said to and for you. There will be enough there to strengthen your faith, for it will be exercised, purified and deepened by the very obscurity of these communications. (2, 8)

This approach is an ever-fresh source of sanctity. It provides us with a way to recognize the manifestation of God and his kingdom in our lives.

Implications for Us

Aelred Squire in his magnificent book *Asking the Fathers* refers to Dorotheus of Gaza.[2] Dorotheus had moved into the desert in Egypt. Apparently before he did so he was accustomed to swimming in the Mediterranean. He described two different ways of swimming in strong current. We can swim directly against the rhythmic movement of the water and find ourselves at times gasping for air as the water breaks over our heads and tires us easily. On the other hand, we can find the inner rhythm of the water and adapt ourselves to it, providing direction with our arms and legs. Dorotheus offers that image to help us grasp the secret for negotiating the challenges of life. We need to find the rhythm of God's will, yield to it while still assuming our own responsibility for preserving the conditions that assist us in responding to him more fully, and therefore find ourselves moving in the direction he wants.

All ascetical effort should lead us to a simpler prayer of the heart. All genuine prayer should lead us to the asceticism that the inner law of love imposes.

[2] See Aelred Squire, *Asking the Fathers* (London: S.P.C.K., 1973), 214–15.

It is ours to recognize the ordinary ways in which God reveals his will. God's will is most fundamentally revealed to us in the concrete circumstances of our responsibilities in life. The commandments of God and the precepts of the Church then provide us with positive universal norms for human behavior. Finally, the inspirations that God provides to us as we reflect on human experience help us to be open and responsive to the Holy Spirit.

Pope Saint John Paul II has offered to us an extraordinary example of what it means to continue to make a gift of self despite facing overwhelming physical diminishment. He was faithful to this self-gift in the face of Nazism, Communism, secularism, and the challenges of serious physical limitations. His interior spirit consistently triumphed over the challenges he experienced. Active self-abandonment enabled his soul to pull his body into a faithful self-gift.

Ultimately, the real obstacles in life are within us rather than outside of us. God can always use an external event, however difficult, to serve his good purpose. All we need to be is receptive and responsive to him. Our ultimate goal in life is to continue to make an ever-fuller return of ourselves to the God who continues to reveal himself to us in the ordinary events of human life until we make the final gift of ourselves to him when he comes at the end of our lives.

Lord Jesus, I believe that you reveal your face in the ordinary events of human life. Yet, I so often fail to recognize you. Help me see and embrace you as you unfold your loving will for me. I want to yield in a profoundly active and cooperative way to the gift of yourself in each person and event. Help me in my weakness. Into your hands I commend my spirit. Amen.

CONCLUSION

This excursion into the Christian spiritual tradition, in an effort to appreciate the wisdom of those who have gone before us and have provided insight into the way God calls us to live life in this world, makes clear for us that there are three basic movements in the living of the Christian spiritual life: conversion of heart, the enlightenment of the mind, and the gift of self.

Conversion of Heart

The desert pioneers taught very clearly that the beginning of Christian discipleship is rooted in the awakening of the desire for God. God has planted this desire within us. We need to uncover and nurture it. For the spiritual life to be truly personal and interior, this desire must continue to be the central motivating reality. Walter Hilton in his *Scale of Perfection* and Jean-Pierre de Caussade in *Abandonment to Divine Providence* reinforced this same truth.

In order for this singleness of desire, or purity of heart, to become more real, we face a need to enter into a purification of the competitive desires that work within us. Although the Christian spiritual life is often referred to as a journey, it is important that we continue to expect a struggle. Otherwise, it is easy for us to take side roads on the pilgrimage and lose our way by trying to avoid conflict. Thomas à Kempis, the author of *The Imitation of Christ*, helped to nudge our attention to the importance of this. Hilton in his systematic treatment, Augustine in his personal witness, and Ignatius of Loyola in his *Spiritual Exercises* challenged us to recognize the seriousness of sin, both personal and social. Moreover, Hilton in a theoretical way and Teresa of Ávila in an experiential way focused on the importance of facing the reality of venial sin as well. Finally, John of the Cross addressed the depths of disorientation that we inherit in our human nature. These disorientations, although not in themselves sinful, need to be faced realistically and exposed to God's redeeming and purifying grace.

Both Benedict and de Caussade highlighted the importance of giving attention to a concrete way of life to support this conversion. Benedict paid attention to the external arrangement of life and then encouraged interior participation in it. De Caussade, while presuming the preservation of basic conditions to support discipleship, revealed to us how critical it is to recognize the way in which God ultimately reveals his will for us in life. He reveals himself in the ordinary events of our life, often in ways that we totally do not expect.

Francis de Sales reminded us of a truth that Teresa of Ávila also treated in a very human way. The cultivation of ordinary virtue has to be the fruit of these efforts. We are not engaged in an exercise of self-perfection. We are called, as Ignatius of Loyola reminded us, to move toward those virtues that support communal life.

The Enlightenment of the Mind

It was after the closure of the period of the early persecutions of the Church and the consequent diminishment of external pressures prompting the disciples of the Lord to take seriously the Christian life that solitaries moved into the desert and helped us recognize the critical importance of solitude. It is only when we can adequately separate ourselves, even for just a short period of time, from the bombardment of messages coming to us from the world, that we begin to introduce into our lives those conditions that open us to God's messages. Guigo the Carthusian repeated this message eight centuries later.

Solitude can never be an end in itself. If it is, it tends to make us eccentric. Basil the Great recognized this in the early hermits and soon brought them together in communal life. As he rightly said, it is only in our interchange with one another that the virtues are tested and that charity can grow.

Solitude then provides a setting for the nurturing of a more receptive attitude toward God. The teaching on prayer contained in the writings of Guigo and Teresa of Ávila make this point. Interior involvement in prayer is the only way in which it can become truly personal. We are taught by God through a prayerful reading of Sacred Scripture, the testimony of the great saints, and the teaching of the Church.

Then this prayer needs to be brought to sacramental encounter. As Catherine of Siena rightly taught, we experience in the Eucharist a particularly efficacious way in which God offers himself as gift and then grants to us a graced capacity to make a return gift to him. It is entering more profoundly into the inner life of worship within the context of the Church's life that we become more formed by the Holy Spirit in the Church. Then we have a sense of how God personalizes his self-revelation to us in the sacrament of the present moment as Jean-Pierre de Caussade taught so effectively.

Since God's revelation is not fundamentally intellectual but the gift of Self, our response to him cannot be merely in the mind or in words. It is to be the return gift of ourselves to him. It is the gift of ourselves back to him for others in imitation of Christ Jesus.

The Gift of Self

The movement into solitude is a condition for becoming more at home with God, with ourselves, and with others. The solitaries of the desert presented this truth in metaphors, parables, and maxims. Aelred of Rievaulx cautioned us that any gift that we make of ourselves in friendship or any pursuit of friendship with others is imperiled if we have not become at home within ourselves and placed God first in life.

It is charity that is the goal of the Christian spiritual life. Each of the spiritual writers we have examined has reinforced the truth that the love of God above all and the love of neighbor as an expression of this love of God is at the heart of the Christian spiritual life. Francis de Sales gave testimony to this in a particularly persuasive way. He identified the varying concentric circles of responsibility that we have in life toward God, toward the members of our own family, toward those with whom we live and work, and then toward those in need. For Aelred of Rievaulx, Christian friendship helps to support, not undermine, these responsibilities of love.

Ultimately, it is the move toward self-oblational love and the ever-increasing gift of ourselves that is important. Jean-Pierre de Caussade insisted on the ultimate gift of ourselves in our abandonment to him. We are called to die to the false self together with Jesus and then rise to the true self in our participation in his Resurrection. But it is in the final analysis God's work in us that makes us holy.

Final Observations

This series of reflections is meant to be simply an introduction to the Christian spiritual teaching present in the patrimony of the Western Church. The selection of the spiritual writers has not been guided by an attempt to be faithful to chronological history, but rather a desire to present in a more systematic way the fundamental realities of the Christian spiritual life. Hence, we have sacrificed the historical approach for a more thematic treatment. The focus has been on the common spiritual teaching in the undivided Church of the West. Hence, the strong emphasis on those writers who either antedated or kept themselves immune from inter-Christian polemic.

It is my hope that this has opened up the possibility of presenting the call of Jesus Christ anew in our own age. The Lord Jesus calls us to encounter him as "the way, and the truth, and the life" (Jn 14:6). He invites us to conversion of heart, enlightenment of mind, and communion with him in love.

I am happy that we can retrieve the classical spiritual literature in our own time in the spirit in which Augustine rediscovered the way to read the *Aeneid*. If we can read the classics and find them to be a mirror in which we see ourselves, both our lights and our shadows, this will help us in the living of the Christian life. If we can see in the spiritual classics the especially graced way in which the Church provides experiential spiritual direction to us, this book will have opened up a very important opportunity.

My desire has been to expound an ecclesial spirituality. The teaching contained here is rooted in Sacred Scripture as unfolded in those spiritual writers who have been recognized by the Church as particularly reliable. We have focused on the *realities* of the Christian life.

Approaching the spiritual patrimony of the Church in this way hopefully enables us to enter into an experience of the Church's spiritual direction. We have tried to touch upon what is common to all people in saying a deeper and fuller yes to the Lord. May God grant that this effort bears fruit according to his loving will.

NAMES INDEX

Note: For a number of reasons this specialized index does not conform to standard indexes. For example, some names appear as they normally would, that is, last names first, followed by first names, while others—particularly saints' names—do not. Another difference is the arbitrary addition of parenthetical material to describe the individual, as in the examples "Mary (Martha's sister)" and "John (the Evangelist)."